The Coming of God's

Arising Generation!

by Pastor Tom Carubba

Published by

SHABAR PUBLICATIONS

www.shabarpublications.com

Most Shabar Publications products are available at special quantity discounts for bulk purchase for sales promotions, fund-raising and educational needs. For details, write Shabar Publications at mayorga1126@gmail.com.

The Coming of God's *Arising* Generation!
by Pastor Tom Carubba

Published by Shabar Publications
3833 N. Taylor Rd.
Palmhurst, Texas 78573
www.shabarpublications.com

Table of Contents

Foreword

Throughout church history, we have seen the *sin and repent and indulge and sin again* cycle of God's people. It seems that there is no end to this wicked cycle.

The problem to all this and why it is such a big deal lies on the fact that *"as the church goes, so goes the world!"*

We saw it in the book of Judges many times over; we saw this cycle in Israel and Judah as they went astray from God's designed plan; and yet God, in His mercy, brought the people back to alignment.

One thing is clear to me, none of these *returns or restorations* happened without *a voice* being raised in the midst of the chaos, the backslidings, the rebelliousness in the heart of God's people.

Though prophets of God paid a hefty price for being God's mouthpiece, they did it anyways! These vessels of God were determined to obey God at any cost. These servants were so dead to their own desires and ambitions, that dying a natural death was a promotion!

It was through their obedience that these servants turned nations around for God. It was because someone heard God and dared to speak and act for Him, that *generations* were saved and restored! Yes, they suffered at the hands of rebellious kings and people; but their words pierced the darkness and restoration was made possible!

I consider Tom Carubba to be one of these prophetic voices for this very hour in this generation without a doubt!

I had not read a book so intense in a good while; and while reading this manuscript, my heart leaped with expectation, as I was challenged and moved within with holy desperation.

Pastor Tom Carubba

To be honest, I said to myself, "This is definitely a voice for the last hour that we are in! It's a heartcry being made in the wilderness of our society, our nation, and for the church of Jesus all over the world."

I know this servant of the Lord personally and have seen his life and have many times heard his cry for revival. It's not a cry of complaint; it is a cry from God's throne to the church in this hour!

Allow these few pages to impact you, as they have impacted me. Thank you Tom for writing these humble notes and sharing them with us.

-David Mayorga
Author of Inextinguishable!

Introduction

What would happen if everyone in the Body of Christ, God's church, understood their own generation? If God's servant would really know exactly what God has in mind for him or her to do in an allotted time frame? Can you imagine how it would affect their service unto the Lord; how to do specific tasks that would bring in the lost; or how much to deepen their hearts and their devotion to Christ, so as to have an impact that would shake their generation?

In Psalm 145 verse 4, the Scripture says, **"One generation shall praise Your works to another; And shall declare Your mighty acts."**

From what I gather, every generation will leave its mark. Throughout time, in the history of humanity, we find men and women who impacted their generations mightily.

The Bible is also filled with many testimonies of men who served God with power and shook their generations. It is my conviction that history will be made by those who are in touch with their generation! I guess I am bringing this to you so that I may ask you: "What kind of mark will you leave in your generation? Have you considered this?

Many want to become a legend. The true Christian wants to leave a legacy; something that is passed on to the next generation.

In this book you will read about the lives of Samson, Joseph, Elijah, Shamgar and many more servants of God who lived and served the Lord in their generation. How were they able to have such an impact? How did they accomplish such great things in their lifetime?

Please note: These were regular ordinary people just like us; the difference was that they came to realize their purpose and calling! This changed everything for them.

My hope is that as you read the pages of this book, your hunger for Jesus will increase; your passion for God will burn deep within; and your outreach vision will be enlarged!

Also, my prayer is that you as one of God's chosen for this generation - will discover, or be empowered (in your already found purpose,) what is the calling that God has specified for you.

Remember: Every generation is needed to fulfill the Great Commission Jesus gave His Church. This means us who believe!

-Tom Carubba, *Senior Pastor*
Hosanna World Changers
Brownsville, Texas

Chapter 1

The Coming of a Generation!

"But this is what was spoken by the prophet Joel:
'And it shall come to pass in the last days, says God, That I
will pour out of My Spirit on all flesh;
Your sons and your daughters shall prophesy, Your young
men shall see visions, Your old
men shall dream dreams.
And on My menservants and on My maidservants I will
pour out My Spirit in those days;
And they shall prophesy.
I will show wonders in heaven above And signs in the
earth beneath: Blood and fire and
vapor of smoke.
The sun shall be turned into darkness, And the moon into
blood, Before the coming
of the great and awesome day of the Lord.
And it shall come to pass that whoever calls on the name
of the Lord." (Acts 2:16-21)

In this moment of history, God has and is still pouring out His Spirit
on His church! His church is you and I laboring with Him in fulfilling
His purpose in our lives.

The Lord leaves no one out; He's pouring out His Spirit on the sons and daughters, young men and old men, menservants and maidservants, everyday people from all walks of life and they shall prophesy.

The Spirit of prophecy should be in each one of us. By the Spirit we are enabled to sense and see things to come and witness the Gospel of Jesus Christ to every man and woman.

The power of God is given regardless of gender (sons and daughters) or age (young and old). All of us can receive divine revelation so that we may declare and communicate to the church, the Body of Christ.

If these things aren't happening in the church today, then the question we have to ask ourselves is, "Who changed things?" Somewhere, somehow, something changed. It changed from a *vibrant, Spirit-empowered, laying hands on the sick and they shall recover, by life or by death faith* type of church; into a *spineless home-and-garden, enjoy the Sunday morning religion show and go home in defeat again* type of church.

Who changed things from **"leave everything and follow Me"** (Luke 14:33,) to "just pray this prayer and you're set for eternity?"

Who changed things from **"all who live godly lives in Jesus will suffer persecution"** (2 Tim. 3:12,) into "ask Jesus into your heart and you'll enjoy a comfortable life?"
Who changed things around from a fearless uncompromised proclamation of the truth at whatever the cost or consequence; to a water down, compromised message that is afraid to offend someone?

Who changed things around, from holiness being beautiful, to holiness being bondage?

Who changed things around from the early church being known for its high standards; to the contemporary church being known for its scandals?

Who changed things around, from a faith that is so focused on the life of Jesus - a life that no sacrifice was considered too great and no act of service too extreme or small? As a matter of fact, when we look at the early church - suffering for Jesus was considered a privilege in comparison to today's *convenience store* Christianity; where we have to sell salvation to the sinner by spicing up the deal with perks and benefits?

In the Reformation of the church, the cry was "Sola Scripture," meaning only the Scriptures. The Scriptures alone are God's Word; and nothing comes after the Scriptures! No traditions, no alleged revelations and no consensus; no new revelations can undermine the written Word of God!

We have to be the generation that knows what God says, and not think *maybe* this is what He said. We need to be the generation that rightly divides the word of truth; that embraces and moves in the true gifts of the Spirit. We must be the generation that not only hear God's voice, but acts on what He said. We need to be the generation, that if Jesus doesn't come in our lifetime - we have prepared the next generation for the coming of Jesus!

"Arise, cry out in the night, At the beginning of the watches; Pour out your heart like water before the face of the Lord. Lift your hands toward Him For the life of your young children, Who faint from hunger at the head of every street." (Lamentations 2:19)

The Prophet Jeremiah was known as the weeping prophet. I would say that when he was writing these words, he was probably writing with a broken heart. Jeremiah had witnessed with his own eyes, all the young people in the streets who had been robbed of true hope and their future. Jeremiah was fully aware that godlessness had infiltrated every aspect of his society.

During this time the people of God lost sight of their spiritual inheritance, choosing to live for themselves in the moment. They allowed the glorious future that was promised to them slip through their fingers.

Think of how heartbreaking it felt for Jeremiah. He knew and understood the desire and promises of God. Jeremiah knew the Lord's purpose for the people who were supposed to be His testimony in the earth at this time.

I can recall the time my wife and I were in New Orleans to visit family. While we were there, we had to go across town by way of driving through the French Quarter seeing multitude of people walking the streets. I was reminded of the Word of God where it talks about how the life of young people faint from hunger at the head of every street. *Faint* meaning that they're shrouded, clothed and overwhelmed in darkness.

All these people we were seeing, and not just them, but all people from all over the place - from every walk of society, no matter what city you may live in; the vast majority of who we were seeing, had been spiritually starved and blinded by the god of this world.

There have been generations here in America that have been raised to believe that there is no God. They are surrounded by a society that attempts to remove everything and anything that has to do with the testimony of Christ. Even sadder than this, is how God's people have dealt casually with the Word of God and have allowed sin to come in. Let me say that sin has bought weakness upon the Church of Jesus Christ today!

Too many Christians have turned inward and started living for themselves. Coming to the house of God, has become more about getting a better career, a business contact, how to develop nicer personality, and how to get ahead in life; and consequently, we started to lose the burden of the Lord.

Unconcerned About Those Coming After Us

It's a dangerous thing if all we're trying to do is ride out the coming storm and not be concerned about those who will follow after us.

"So Hezekiah said to Isaiah, "The word of the Lord which you have spoken is good!" For he said, "Will there not be peace and truth at least in my days?" (2 Kings 20:19)

King Hezekiah was a king who had once known the presence and power of God, but when he received his word from the Lord telling him that a day is soon coming when everything he has, even his sons, would be taken from him and taken prisoner to Babylon, all he could say was, **"Will there not be peace and truth at least in my days?"**

Think about what Hezekiah is saying here: "As long as none of this happens in my lifetime; and as long as I can keep my stuff and my possessions, I'm OK with it; let the next generation worry about it."

Is it a tragic statement to make; so long as it's not happening to us, let others worry about it!

When my wife and I rode down that street in New Orleans, it was as if we were witnessing a modern day Sodom and Gomorrah; nothing was hidden, nothing behind closed doors; everything was right out there in the open for all to see. I also noticed that parents with young children, were walking as if this was all normal.

On many people we could see the look of vacancy, a look of emptiness, they're trying to satisfy a look of death. They're been left to wander the streets searching for bits of reality and meaning to give them a future. Some of them are venting their anger through protest and being anti-establishment, trying to find a *just* society; which by the way, they will never find apart from Jesus Christ!

If the church would not have watered-down the Word of God or denied the truth of the Gospel that Jesus saves, heals, delivers, restores, and gives us life with a purpose, all these generations would know where the true power of God is, and would be a force to be reckon with.

When Someone Rises Up!

There was another time when the people of God were being afflicted and their children were being gripped by the enemy.

"Then the king of Egypt spoke to the Hebrew midwives, of whom the name of one was Shiphrah and the name of the other Puah; and he said, "When you do the duties of a midwife for the Hebrew women, and see them on the birthstools, if it is a son, then you shall kill him; but if it is a daughter, then she shall live." (Exodus 1:15-16)

Pharaoh even went on to say that every son that is born will be thrown in the river; and every daughter that is born will be allowed to live. The Israelite male children were being throw into the river to drown, to die, a physical picture of what is happening in our generation as young people have been cast out into a river of confusion.

If we don't think there's confusion, just think for a minute how so many don't know what true marriage is; they don't know when the life of a baby starts; and not to mention all the confusion regarding their gender.

When we see this picture, we might think all is hopeless; we may think the enemy has completely taken captive this generation, but the time came when one of God's people rose up. God will always have a REM-NANT.

You know the story: there was a man and wife and the wife became pregnant. She delivered a son and hid him for three months, but when she couldn't hide him any longer she put him in a basket and put it in the reeds by the river's bank. (Ex.2:1-3)

This woman defied everything that was coming against her and her family and put the child in the mercy of God.

There is always someone, who throughout history will rise up and declare, "NO devil, you are not getting my children. Not on my watch. I know the Living God."
When this woman put this child in that basket, there was no way she could have known what the fullness of the impact that her choice would make for the Israelite nation. She didn't understand that this child, Moses, would be the one who would eventually deliver his people out of bondage.

Years later, the day came when Moses came and stood before Pharaoh's throne. He wasn't carrying a sword, he wasn't wearing any armor, but he had all he needed, a staff in his hand and confidence in his God.

There was Moses standing before Pharoah, the mightiest man in the world and said, "Let my people go. I'm not making any deals with you. We're all going – our young are going, our old are going, our children are going. Everything that belongs to the children of God is going. No one will be left behind – NOT ON MY WATCH."

Righteous Indignation!

Just like Moses, righteous indignation must arise in each one of our hearts in this day and time. As lawlessness abounds and our nation is being devoured by ungodliness and perversion, we don't have time to wait for another superstar preacher to rise up!

I thank God for the mighty men and women who have gone before us and have set the example; but now is the time for the weak, the foolish, the nobodies and the nothings, to press into the Throne room of God.

God is not looking for the most qualified person or the person who has it all together. He's looking for people with hearts of faith; those who believe that if God said it, that's enough for me! Yes, God is looking for those who come to His Throne, not with their own strategies, but with a heart that simply believes, "God, I know that You are good and that Your mercy endures forever."

Think about it: When God wanted to bring a prophet to the nation, He looked for a barren womb in a woman called Hannah. When God wanted to deliver His people from the Midianites, He showed Himself to Gideon, the least in his father's house. When God made a promise to Abraham that his descendants would be as numerous as the stars, God waited until Abraham had no possible way of doing it in his own strength.

The Lord is waiting for ordinary people like you and me to discover His heart! The heart of God is for men and women to be reconciled back to Him and to become all that God has created and destined them to be. He is looking for a people who lay hold of the things that are not in their grasp yet, but by faith, have understanding of truths which the natural minds can't comprehend; a people who live in the freedom that only Jesus can bring.

God is waiting for us to come to Him and say, *"God, I have discovered something about Your heart. I know You are a God who does miracles and I know also that You are merciful. Therefore, I'm coming on behalf of the children of this generation. I'm speaking for those who have been robbed, those who have been left behind, those who have been wounded, those who are fainting and dying because I have in some way denied them access to You, the Living God. You are merciful to my failings and You will be merciful to this generation! Help me Lord to understand who You are and who I am in You."*

"Arise, cry out in the night, At the beginning of the watches; Pour out your heart like water before the face of the Lord. Lift your hands toward Him For the life of your young children, Who faint from hunger at the head of every street." (Lamentation 2:19)

Church, it's time to pray - to pray for the future generations. The rising up of the next generations depends upon this generation crying out in prayer before God. It isn't right that *the godless* have control over our children and young people. It isn't right that our schools, which are supposed to be places of intellectual discussion, have become places of indoctrination and mockery.

We, the church, the believers, the disciples of Jesus Christ, have the power to position our young people for a season of incredible mercy.

How do I know this? Because it is promised in His Word:
"Behold, I will send you Elijah the prophet Before the coming of the great and dreadful day of the Lord." And he will turn The hearts of the fathers to the children, And the hearts of the children to their fathers, Lest I come and strike the earth with a curse." (Malachi 4:5, 6)

God is raising up grandmothers, grandfathers, Maw-Maw's and Paw-Paw's, mothers and fathers, pastors and ordinary people who simply have a heart for God. It is this cry, that will turn the hearts of the fathers to the children and the hearts of the children to the fathers. God will turn back the hearts of those who are spiritual fathers and mothers; but first you and I have to be a people of prayer!

The Apostle Paul wrote to the church and firmly affirmed that he knew in whom he had believed; and that he was persuaded that He (God) was able to keep that which he had committed to Him. Therefore you and I can believe the same thing for our children, grandchildren, brothers, sisters and parents – NO ONE LEFT BEHIND!

We, the Church of Jesus Christ, are in a moment of time where something incredible can happen in this nation. It has the potential to be incredible one way or the other - incredibly dark or incredibly lit.

There's a coming generation and the generation is already here. This generation is rising up, not only in this nation, but all over the world. They won't quit, they won't back down, they can't be bought and they will keep pressing in!

We're in a moment where you and I must make a choice; a choice to rise up and pray. We must ask God to forgive us for what we have done and for what we haven't done; for handling the great truth of His Word casually,and for the lack of prayer in His house, which by the way, Jesus said, **"My house shall be called a house of prayer."**

It's time to believe for this generation that **"whoever calls upon the name of the Lord shall be saved,"** and let us once again, witness God's miracles and mercy in our day!

Chapter 2

The Shamgar Generation:
Enough Is Enough! Generation

Before we get to Shamgar, this is what has happened in the nation of Israel: God's deliverer Ehud, killed Eglon who was the leader of the Moabites. This man oppressed God's people for years. After Ehud killed Eglon, the nation of Israel rose up and defeated the nation of Moab by killing ten thousand of Moab's mighty men. After the defeat, the nation of Israel had rest for eight years.

"So Moab was subdued that day under the hand of Israel. And the land had rest for eighty years. After him was Shamgar the son of Anath (answer), who killed six hundred men of the Philistines with an ox goad; and he also delivered Israel." (Judges 3:30-31)

"In the days of Shamgar, son of Anath, In the days of Jael, The highways were deserted, and the travelers walked along the by-ways." (Judges 5:6)

The *highways* were well-travelled roads, a smooth path; these were roads that caravans could travel on. Now, the *byways*, were crooked ways, they were rougher; they were roads of uneven surface, not really roads of comfortable travel.
It says the *highways* were deserted - think about that for a moment.

In the United States of America, we have casinos open and churches closed and deserted. In major cities in America, there are churches whose doors haven't opened for months – while abortion clinics – liquor stores are considered essential.

We can turn on our television or search the internet and see thousands of people rioting and setting fires to private and government property throughout our city streets. There are those who say they have a right to do those things, but in the same breath, they say that churches have to close because of people being too close to each other and singing.

Let's look at this man named Shamgar: During the days of Shamgar the land was infested with robbers and plunderers; people couldn't travel the well-travelled roads because they would be in danger of being attacked - the people were forced to take shelter and hide.

I can remember when I got saved back in the 1970's; the attitude of some in the church was, *let us circle the wagons and hold on until Jesus comes!*

We can look at much of the church today and the attitude is, *let's not cause too much trouble – let's be tolerant - let's not say too much, and they'll leave us alone, and we can go back to having church!"*

This isn't what God had intended His church to do. God is looking to raise up deliverers; He always has a people, a group of called-out believers who will not bow, not bend a knee to society; a people who are not silent, a people that will say ENOUGH IS ENOUGH!

When you look at the passages of the Bible concerning Shamgar, much is not said except for the two opening verses we read in the beginning of this chapter - that would be Judges chapter 3, verses 30 and 31, and Judges chapter 5, verse 6.

Shamgar is not mentioned in the heroes of faith in the Book of Hebrews; we don't know how long or how many days he travelled the *byways*. Now, what we do know, is that one day, he made a choice to bypass the byways and take the highway road; he ended up killing six hundred Philistines with an ox goad.

An ox goad is a strong pole about eight feet long and two inches in diameter. At one end was a sharp point for pricking the oxen when their movements became too slow; at the other end of the ox goad, was a sharp chisel-like blade, which was used to clear the plowshare of weeds, roots or thorns.

Just like Shamgar, there is a generation of believers who are looking at what is going on in society and are saying ENOUGH IS ENOUGH! It's time to take a stand, it's time to raise a voice, it's time to fight and give it all to the Lord!
Those Who Will Say *Enough Is Enough.*

Depending on how old you are, you might remember the catch phrase from Popeye the Sailor Man, *I've done stand all I can stand, and I can't stand no more.*

In Matthew 21, Jesus goes into the temple and turns the money tables over and drives out all those who were selling merchandise, saying, **"My house shall be called a house of prayer, but you have made it a den of thieves."** It's as if Jesus was saying, "ENOUGH IS ENOUGH! - no more of this! Out you go! This is MY house, not your house; hit the door!"

Could it be that Jesus is speaking to His church today and saying - enough with the games, the going through the motions, the gimmicks, the hype. It is time to get back to the place where people would come into God's house and say, **"We would see Jesus!"**

We're living in a time where people are looking for Jesus; not a hype-up Jesus, not a super hip cool Jesus; but a Jesus who is real, a Jesus who knows what it's like in the real world! They are looking for a Jesus that saves, heals, and delivers; a Jesus that can take broken-down lives, and make them new; a Jesus who can give peace in the midst of chaos.

Enough With Idols And Double-Mindedness!
"And Elijah came to all the people, and said, "How long will you falter between two opinions (divided mind)? If the Lord is God, follow Him; but if Baal, follow him." But the people answered him not a word." (1 Kigns 18:21)

This is the Prophet Elijah confronting the prophets of Baal; and while confronting them he tells the people of Israel to make up their minds and determine who the real God is.

In James 1, the Apostle James states that a man who is double-minded is unstable in all his ways. Unstable is being two-spirited in opinion and purpose. Double-minded, two-spirited in opinion, two-faced.

Is this not what we're seeing in political parties in our generation – going back and forth saying things that are not true - all for votes? It's like saying, "I'm for whatever you are for: if you like it, I like it; if you don't like it, I don't like it."

God is saying to a generation – "How long are you going to keep going back and forth? Make up your mind: If God be God, then say it and live it!"

Enough With Doubt

Doubt is being uncertain, unsure, or not knowing what is real. I got to admit that at times, I have had a hard time with this one. I guess it's because my name is Thomas, like the disciple Thomas who was known for doubting. Remember, it was Thomas who said, **"Unless I see it, unless I touch it, I will not believe it."**

"But without faith it is impossible (unable) **to please Him, for he who comes to God must believe that He is, and that He is a rewarder of those who diligently** (to search out, investigate, crave) **seek Him."** (Hebrews 11:6)

We need to quit doubting God and doubting His Word. We must come to Him with child-like faith believing Him for the impossible; to know that He meets all our needs. He will open doors that need to be opened and close doors that need to be closed.

With everything going on today, it's hard to see and witness what's going on around us and think that God has it all under control. You see doubt comes in and we start to wonder if God is seeing what's happening in society and in the Church world? One thing I know about doubt: If God said it, then it is true; if God said it, then it stands!

Enough With *Worshiptainment*!

You and I are to worship God and not worship entertainment. The lie and heresy of the church is that the church thinks they are in the entertainment business. A. W. Tozer stated in the 1960's – *"Church members want to be entertained while they are edified; it's scarcely possible in most places to get anyone to attend a meeting where the only attraction was God."*

It's become sad to see worship services becoming more and more of a pep rally atmosphere. Now there's nothing wrong with excitement - the Word of God tells us there's singing in the house of the Lord, there's leaping, lifting hands, shouting, praising God, - but when we depend upon props more than on the presence of God, WE HAVE BECOME WORSHIPTAINMENT.

Now understand, it's not about worship styles. It's not about traditional worship versus contemporary worship, and it's not about organs versus drums. What real worship really is: It's about the heart, the focus, and the intent of worship. You have to ask, *"On who or on what is the spotlight on?"* If it's on anything or on anyone else apart from God - then it's not the worship God intended!

Enough with worshiptainment! The message of the church isn't *come and have a good time*; the message should be *the cross of Christ*. We are called to pick up the cross and follow Jesus!

Enough With Conformity!

"I beseech you therefore, brethren, by the mercies of God, that you present your bodies a living sacrifice, holy, acceptable to God, which is your reasonable service. And do not be conformed (fashioned, pattern) **to this world, but be transformed by the renewing of your mind, that you may prove what is that good and acceptable and perfect will of God."** (Romans 12:1, 2)

There are some who are starting to conform, starting to bend, and starting to surrender to the ways of the world. Churches that have used phrases like "Black Lives Matter" or "White silence is violence," - they've already giving in to those who hate God.

Many church leaders think that by saying those things or supporting them, will be exempt from the mob; they are mistaken! They have fooled themselves. These are God-haters and they hate everything and anything that has to with God.

We are not to be conformed to his world; not to pattern or fashion ourselves after this world. It's like when Paul told Timothy, that in the last days there will be those who have a form of godliness, but they deny the power. Enough with conformity! It's time for the church to push back on the lies of the enemy.

Are we ready to go above the norm, above the ordinary; and to become those who walk in victory - even if it means walking the road alone?

"Then Jesus came with them to a place called Gethsemane, and said to the disciples, "Sit here while I go and pray over there." And He took with Him Peter and the two sons of Zebedee, and He began to be sorrowful and deeply distressed. Then He said to them, "My soul is exceedingly sorrowful, even to death. Stay here and watch with Me." He went a little farther and fell on His face, and prayed, saying, "O My Father, if it is possible, let this cup pass from Me; nevertheless, not as I will, but as You will." Then He came to the disciples and found them sleeping, and said to Peter, "What! Could you not watch with Me one hour?" (Matthew 26:36-40)

Jesus was alone in the midst of His most difficult hour and time of His life, and His closest friends are sleeping. Some of the greatest victories that you and I will win, will not be in a crowd, but when we are by ourselves alone with God.

Picture the scene: You have Shamgar walking through the *byways*, it's hot with no breeze and the ground isn't smooth; Shamgar is hot, tired, and frustrated. Shamgar looks and sees the *highways*, the smooth and flat places, but he knows those roads are the most dangerous since the Philistines travel and occupy those roads.

As Shamgar is walking down the rough road, something comes over him; something inside of him rises up and he says to himself, *Today, this day, I walk the highway and this day no one better get in my way.*

May the church together with you and me, rise up to the occasion and say, *I'm going through, devil look out, I'm not turning around nor going back, this is my road, this is my family, this is my home, and this is my Church!*

We must also come to the realization that the road we are on, is the road that God has for us; and that road is our road, no one else's! It's for us and for us alone.

Is there something within you that says "enough?" If the answer is *yes*, then be the generation to walk your road!

Chapter 3

The Joseph Generation:
A Type Of Christ

"Now Israel loved Joseph more than all his children, because he was the son of his old age. Also he made him a tunic of many colors. But when his brothers saw that their father loved him more than all his brothers, they hated him and could not speak peaceably to him. Now Joseph had a dream, and he told it to his brothers; and they hated him even more. So he said to them, "Please hear this dream which I have dreamed: There we were, binding sheaves in the field. Then behold, my sheaf arose and also stood upright; and indeed your sheaves stood all around and bowed down to my sheaf." And his brothers said to him, "Shall you indeed reign over us? Or shall you indeed have dominion over us?" So they hated him even more for his dreams and for his words. Then he dreamed still another dream and told it to his brothers, and said, "Look, I have dreamed another dream. And this time, the sun, the moon, and the eleven stars bowed down to me." So he told it to his father and his brothers; and his father rebuked him and said to him, "What is this dream that you have dreamed? Shall your mother and I and your brothers indeed come to bow down to the earth before you?" And his brothers envied (jealous of, envious of) him, but his father kept the matter in mind." (Genesis 37:3-11)

Most know that Joseph is a type of Christ, but he's also a type of the last day's remnant, a generation that is part of the original, a group of people that God is and has raised up to show His church how to break out of a spiritual famine.

The Joseph Generation is a body of believers who are given totally over to the Lord. These believers commune with the Lord daily; they are led by the Spirit of God; and in the days we are living in right now, they are coming out of great trials and great testing.

The Joseph Generation is entering into a place of revelation, wisdom and fruitfulness. God is working in them and through them. God is giving them His truth and knowledge.

There have always been generations in history ...

The Greatest Generation – 1901 through 1927 (this generation is known as the G.I. Generation and World War 2 Generation, this generation lived through the Great Depression).

The Silent Generation – 1927 through 1946 (children to be seen and not heard.)

The Baby Boomers Generation – 1946 through 1964

Generation X – 1965 through 1980

Millennials – 1981 through 1996

Generation Z – 1997 through 2012

In the Bible you have –

a Moses Generation that led God's people out of captivity;

a Joshua Generation that led God's people into the Promise Land;

a Samson Generation who are the fighters of God's enemies;

a David Generation who are the worshippers, the ones after God's heart;

a Solomon Generation who are the builders of God's House.

The definition of *generation* is an entire body of individuals born and living at about the same time; a group of individuals belonging to a specific category at the same time.

God is raising up a Joseph Generation for the times we are living in. You can realize and see that much of the church of Jesus Christ has grown sensual, worldly, wicked, and cold.

In Mathew 24, Jesus tells His disciples the signs of His coming. Jesus said that there would be wars and rumors of wars, false Christs, nation would rise against nation, famines, pestilences, earthquakes; He said that many would be offended; there would be betrayals of one another, and false prophets. Jesus goes on to say that because lawlessness (that is wickedness,) unrighteousness would abound, and that the love of many would grow cold.

The mentality of some churches is to circle the wagons and shut the world out and hold on! That's not Jesus' church! His Church is a LIGHT to the world and SALT to the earth. We're to give light in a dark and cold world and give flavor to people who have a bitter taste from what society has trapped them in.

Then we will have the other churches who will not say anything of the sins that plague our society and the future of our children. We will never hear them mention anything against perversion, abortion, same-sex marriage. I believe that the reason why they are so quiet on the subjects is because they say they want to be *inclusive*. In other words, "Tell of the love of God; no judgement; let them know that God accepts them as they are!"

What's God's answer to a church that is backslidden and in famine? God is always at work way in advance in His church. God has always moved ahead and prepares a way out for His people.

The members of Israel's family, Joseph's father's family, would have died because of famine if it wasn't for God's plan ahead of time. God had a plan to save His people from destruction.

God sent Joseph ahead to Egypt 20 years before the famine. During those 20 years, God was working in Joseph; isolating him, trying him, and preparing him for a place of authority. The reason for those years were because Joseph was to become the life saver of God's people.

God kept Joseph from the spotlight of popularity to be trained and ready for the coming day of chaos and death, ready for the day of famine.

Just like God isolated Joseph, God has a Joseph Generation hidden today. This generation is in the furnace of affliction, in battlegrounds of trials and temptation; yes, this generation is dying to self!

Let me also add that this generation wants nothing of fame or popularity. It simply keeps growing hungrier to have more of Jesus, more of His presence, to know His voice and His heart.

You may know of someone, or it might be you, who like Joseph, God has given dreams and promises concerning your own life, your family, your call. You may not understand all the testings, trials, circumstances, situations and troubles in your life at this time; but rest assured, that God has a purpose for all this. God is making you into a Joseph Generation!

There are a few things that Joseph had to go through to become a "tried and tested" servant of God. If you truly have a desire and want to be a part of this generation, you will encounter and experience these too.

Spirit's Call to a Holy and Separated Life

Joseph responded to the Spirit's call to a holy and separated life. Throughout the Word of God and history, the Spirit of God calls men and women to holiness, purity of heart and a separated life.

Joseph responded to God's call at an early age. Joseph's ten brothers received the same call, the call to surrender, to walk righteously and separate themselves; but they chose to remain in the world. Their decision was pretty much based upon their half-heartedness toward the things of God.

There was two occasions when all of Jacob's (Israel) sons received the Spirit's call to a separated life ...

"And he bought the parcel of land, where he had pitched his tent, from the children of Hamor, Shechem's father, for one hundred pieces of money. Then he erected an altar there and called it El Elohe Israel." (Genesis 33:19-20)

In Schechem, Jacob built an altar to the God of Israel. Jacob called his sons to the altar to worship with him, to kneel before the Lord and follow the Lord; but Joseph's brothers turned to revenge when their sister Dinah was defiled by a Shechemite. They attacked the city, burned it down and killed every man, woman and child.

The ten brothers didn't give themselves to trust and serve God; and because of that, their violence made Jacob to "stink" among the Canaanites.

"Then Jacob said to Simeon and Levi, "You have troubled me by making me obnoxious (stink, made to be an abomination) among the inhabitants of the land, among the Canaanites and the Perizzites; and since I am few in number, they will gather themselves to-

gether against me and kill me. I shall be destroyed, my household and I." (Genesis 34:30)

"Then God said to Jacob, "Arise, go up to Bethel and dwell there; and make an altar there to God, who appeared to you when you fled from the face of Esau your brother." And Jacob said to his household and to all who were with him, "Put away the foreign gods that are among you, purify yourselves, and change your garments. Then let us arise and go up to Bethel; and I will make an altar there to God, who answered me in the day of my distress and has been with me in the way which I have gone." Genesis 35:1-3)

Changing your garments means a moral and spiritual purification of mind and heart. If you keep reading, verse 4, it says that Joseph's brothers gave up all the strange gods that they had; but this was just an outwardly show, superficial, symbolism over substance; their repentance was only a surface repentance; they never had a true heart change, they returned to their rebellion, hate and envy.

There was something different about Joseph. His repentance was from the heart, he responded to the Spirit's call. Joseph from the age of 17 determined to follow the Lord; to follow the Lord even in the midst of a wicked and evil society. He determined to have clean hands and a pure heart.

In our lives, the truth of the matter is that, a change of heart has to be followed by a change of habit. If there is no change of habit, then there is no change of heart!

Remember when the Lord sent Samuel to the house of Jesse to anoint the new king of Israel? When Samuel saw Jesse's oldest son Eliab, Samuel said, **"Surely the Lord's anointed is before Him, but God told Samuel to not look at the appearance or at the physical stature, for I the Lord don't see as man sees, man looks on the outward, but I look at the heart."**

Everything can look good on the outside. A church can have what can be considered the best location on a main highway, the best parking lot, the biggest auditorium and the latest technology, the biggest screens; but God is looking for the place where He is welcomed and worshipped; not a place where He's just wanted for a visit! God wants to inhabit, set up residence!

"Now Jacob dwelt in the land where his father was a stranger, in the land of Canaan. This is the history of Jacob. Joseph, being seventeen years old, was feeding the flock with his brothers. And the lad was with the sons of Bilhah and the sons of Zilpah, his father's wives; and Joseph brought a bad report of them to his father. Now Israel loved Joseph more than all his children, because he was the son of his old age. Also he made him a tunic (coat) of many colors. But when his brothers saw that their father loved him more than all his brothers, they hated him and could not speak peaceably to him." (Genesis 37:1-4)

Joseph's father made him a special coat that made him stand out among his brothers.

Let's ask a question: Does God favor some people over others? Doesn't the Bible say that God is no respecter of persons? The answer would be YES it does say that - when it comes to the subject of salvation and His promises.

Now, God treats us all alike; but what we must know, is that God also responds to everyone who responds wholeheartedly to His calling. God's special favor is on those who yield their lives to Him entirely!

"You have granted me life and favor, And Your care has preserved my spirit." (Job 10:12)

"For You, O Lord, will bless the righteous; With favor You will surround him as with a shield." (Psalm 5:12)

"I will greatly rejoice in the Lord, My soul shall be joyful in my God; For He has clothed me with the garments of salvation, He has covered me with the robe of righteousness …" (Isaiah 61:10)

Joseph responded to the Spirit's call, and he received favor from his father. Joseph was given a robe that set him apart, but that favor cost him. That favor brought him rejection, misunderstanding, and ridicule. His brothers hated him for it!

Why did Joseph's brothers turn on him? The reason was that when they saw Joseph wearing the robe, it showed favor and righteousness.

They hated it [the coat of many colors,] because it reminded them of how they rejected the Spirit's call. Joseph's brothers were more occupied and concerned about possessions, material things, and fortune.

There will always be people who want to talk about their cars, their houses, jobs, the places they have been, the latest fashions, and the people they hang out with - and though those things are not bad things, they simply don't interest those who are of the Joseph Generation.

The Joseph Generation is a different level, a different dimension; this generation is hearing from God. The Lord is showing them dreams and visions.

Joseph's Greatest Trial Was the Word of God That He Trusted

"He sent a man before them — Joseph — who was sold as a slave. They hurt his feet with fetters, He was laid in irons. Until the time that his word came to pass, The word of the Lord tested (refined, purged) him." (Psalm 105:17-19)

It states that God Himself sent a man called Joseph to Egypt as a slave - but how did Joseph go to Egypt?

Remember God sent him there to be able to save his family. God sent him there not as an ambassador, but as a slave; as someone without any prospect of hope of ever being free.

Then Joseph after being a slave in a household, God brings him lower. Joseph now becomes a prisoner in Pharaoh's dungeon. It says that his feet hurt as they put irons on his feet to walk around in every day he was there.

God's Word tried Joseph - the Word of God tried his faith and patience. There was a set season, a set time for God's Word to come to pass. Habaakkuk 2 says, **"For the vision is yet for an appointed time; But at the end it will speak, and it will not lie."**

For an *appointed time* is a set time; a due season time. That's why we're told to not grow weary while doing good, for in due season we will reap, if we don't faint and lose heart.

When it was time, God made a way for Joseph to be called before Pharaoh and Joseph was sent for. Joseph was loosed from his imprisonment and was made second in charge of all of Egypt.

We need to not lose hope; we're not to give up our faith. The day is coming when it's all going to be put together. You'll see it come to pass and make sense and then realize it was worth it all.

Think about what Joseph endured at 17 years old. He was thrown into a pit by his brothers; he was sold by his brothers to Ishmaelite traders and taken down to Egypt to be sold as a slave. Now in all those things that were happening, that *still* wasn't his greatest of trials; his greatest trial was the Word of God.

God revealed to Joseph through dreams that he would be given great authority; that he would use that authority for God's glory. His brothers would bow down before him, and that he would be a deliverer of many people.

Everything that happened in Joseph's life was just the opposite of what God had said, JOSEPH WAS THE SERVANT – HE WAS THE ONE BOWING.

Joseph, for ten years, served in Potiphar's house faithfully. Even when Potiphar's wife tempted him, he refused the temptation, and did nothing wrong. He was still thrown in the dungeon of Pharaoh. Can you picture Joseph thinking to himself, "Did I hear right? Did I let pride come in and dreamed these dreams myself? Could my brothers have been right? Maybe these things are happening to me as some kind of punishment."

Doesn't it seem that when we decide to ompletely be sold out to the Lord, to completely follow Him and all His ways, ALL HELL BREAKS LOOSE? This is what is meant by being tried by the Word of God!

In the midst of all the trials and hard places, God prospers His Joseph Generation! While Joseph was a servant in Potiphar's house, he was blessed by God. Even when Joseph found himself in jail; God prospered him there too.

You might be asking, "How did God prosper Joseph?" It wasn't with money, possessions. or some kind of position; God prospered Joseph's spirit. God was speaking to his heart, giving him dreams and interpretations.

Joseph had faith; and that in spite of all the hardships and situations that were beyond his control, GOD WAS WITH HIM!

God is a Father and as a father myself, I know that God probably wanted to tell Joseph that it was all going to work out; it's going to be alright; but Joseph was still in school.

If we are part of the Joseph Generation, then we are learning to lean on God in our trials, learning to trust God completely and not complain.

We may not understand why things are happening around us; things that are the opposite of what God had told us. The Joseph Generation understands that God's wisdom is attained by trials, tribulations, hardships and testings. We don't pray down wisdom, we live it out!

The Day Comes When Everything Makes Sense

God brought everything together and every word and promise was fulfilled. There's Joseph sitting in a jail cell, when all of a sudden there's a commotion in the prison hallways; the guards come in and tell Joseph to get cleaned up, "Pharaoh is calling for you!"

Joseph is cleaned up and now is standing before Pharaoh listening to his dream. Joseph gave the interpretation of the coming famine and then told Pharaoh to gather and store the nation's grain.

"Now therefore, let Pharaoh select a discerning and wise man,

and set him over the land of Egypt." (Genesis 41:33)

"And Pharaoh said to his servants, "Can we find such a one as this, a man in whom is the Spirit of God?" Then Pharaoh said to Joseph, "Inasmuch as God has shown you all this, there is no one as discerning and wise as you. You shall be over my house, and all my people shall be ruled according to your word; only in regard to the throne will I be greater than you." And Pharaoh said to Joseph, "See, I have set you over all the land of Egypt." (Genesis 41:38-41)

Think of how quickly things can change. Within a few hours, Joseph had gone from being an unknown prisoner to the second most powerful man in Egypt. Fast forward a little: the day came when Joseph stood before his brothers and was able to say, **"But as for you, you meant evil against me; but God meant it for good, in order to bring it about as it is this day, to save many people alive."** (Genesis 50:20)

"For His anger is but for a moment, His favor is for life; Weeping may endure for a night. But joy comes in the morning." (Psalm 30:5)

Jesus spoke the words in the Gospel of John chapter 16, **"A woman, when she is in labor, has sorrow because her hour has come; but as soon as she has given birth to the child, she no longer remembers the anguish, for joy that a human being has been born into the world."**

Know this: If we are part of this Joseph Generation, very soon we are going to understand the trials that we've been through or are presently going through. God is going to bring us into the promise He gave us; and just like Joseph, IT WILL ALL MAKE SENSE!

We will be able to say, "Now I know why all the sleepless nights; now I know why all the tears, the heartaches, the loneliness, the rejections, the misunderstandings - it is as if God orchestrated everything." At this point we will see that God has never forsaken us. We will see and understand how God all along had been training us, preparing us, and teaching us to trust Him in everything.

God has planned a time for us to be used; to be brought up to the forefront. That time is just around the corner. The greatest evangelists will not be in the pulpit, but in the congregation!

How are we responding to God's dealings in our life? Are we persuaded that God is at work in all things concerning us?

"And we know that all things (everything, whatever things) work together for good to those who love God, to those who are the called according to His purpose." (Romans 8:28)

Let us hold on to our faith! We will come out of the fire like an honorable vessel to do God's will; yes, as part of the Joseph Generation!

Chapter 4

The Issachar Generation:
Understanding the Times

"And God listened to Leah, and she conceived and bore Jacob a fifth son. Leah said, "God has given me my wages, because I have given my maid to my husband." So she called his name Issachar (He will reward)." (Genesis 30:17-18)

In the Book of Genesis chapter 49, we have the record of Jacob telling all his sons his last words and what the future will hold for each one of them. To Issachar, Jacob's words were, **"Issachar is a strong donkey, lying down between two burdens; He saw that rest was good, And that the land was pleasant; He bowed his shoulder to bear a burden, And became a band of slaves."** (Genesis 49:14-15)

One translation has it that Issachar is one tough donkey and if you think about it, weren't we all tough and stubborn like mules before we came to Jesus? As a matter of fact, there are some who are still tough.

Please note this: When Issachar saw how pleasant the country was, he gave up his freedom and went to work as a slave.

Paul wrote to the church in Rome that we have been set free from sin and now have become slaves of God with fruit to holiness and everlasting life. (Romans 6:22)

When you and I see that serving the Lord is good and that the promises of God are pleasant, it should make our everyday service to the Lord easier, and encourage us to go on despite the hardships. Charles Spurgeon said in his last sermon to the young men and women in his service, that if they really understood the goodness of God, they would rush to be enlisted in His service!

"Now their brethren among all the families of Issachar were mighty men of valor, listed by their genealogies, eighty-seven thousand in all." (1 Chronicles 7:5)

The men of Issachar were valiant men, powerful men, champions, and warriors; they pressed into the fight, they didn't run, didn't retreat, they charged forward.

In 1 Chronicles chapter 12, it records, **"...of the sons of Issachar who had understanding, knowledge, wisdom of the times to know what Israel ought to do."**

The anointing of Issachar caused them to understand the times and seasons to influence and to lead Israel in establishing the greatest kingdom of all Israel's history - King David's kingdom; which is a type and shadow to come of Jesus' Kingdom.

The sons of Issachar studied and analyzed the times they were living in. They understood the times. It was obvious to them that Saul was and would not, be a good king for them and the nation.

We're living in a time where the church, (God's true church, which is you and I,) need to understand *what to do*. I do believe all of us can agree that we are living in such difficult times.

We need a generation of Issachar's to demonstrate to the church, what it is that it's supposed to accomplish, to represent, to speak, what it is to sacrifice, and what it is to represent in this moment of history.

Daniel Boone, the great frontiersman, was asked one time, "Mr. Boone, have you ever been lost?" To which he replied, "Well I was once bewildered for four days, but I've never been lost." That may sound funny, but it is a statement of some certainty. For an experienced explorer and frontiersman like Daniel Boone, it would be next to impossible for him to be actually lost in a true sense, for he was a man of resources, initiative, and skill.

It didn't matter in what area of wilderness or frontier Daniel Boone was in, he still had the confidence of his skills and wilderness survival knowledge. It didn't matter if he found himself in mountains, valleys or swamps during the winter, summer, spring or fall, it made no difference to him. His knowledge, experience and skills served to keep him alive and on a correct heading. North was still north, and south was still south, and that would never change. He knew what to do in any season or location, no matter what the occasion brought. He lived to tell the story time and again.

God's Purpose Never Changes

God's purpose and His will never change. His purposes are truer than *true north* and more certain than the directions on a compass. If we know His Word and His purposes in this season, in this day, in this time period of history - there isn't any reason that we should give up, retreat, quit, and/or be defeated.

"But we have this treasure in earthen vessels, that the excellence of the power may be of God and not of us. We are hard-pressed on every side, yet not crushed; we are perplexed, but not in despair; persecuted, but not forsaken; struck down, but not destroyed." (2 Corinthians 4:7-9)

In the midst of all the things that are happening around us, God has not left our side. He has not abandoned us; yes, there are times when we don't know what to do, but God knows what to do! It's been said that one of the doctrines of the *Navy Seals* is that when they go into battle, the only way you can be defeated, is to give up or be dead.

Like the *Navy Seals*, we do not let circumstances determine who we are or what we know. Those things might affect our attitude or willingness, but we still make the choices regardless.

We may be bewildered for a few days, but who we know, and who we are, will get us through the bewildering places and times!

Understanding the Times

In this moment of history that we are living in, there must be those who can, by skill and impartation, be able to read and understand the times; yes, understand the political winds that are blowing across our nation and the world; to discern the difference between a genuine move of God and a fad passing through. Those, who like the sons of Issachar, understood the times with the knowledge of what Israel should do.

Those who are of this generation, the generation of Issachar: their voice is a voice that is needed, a voice that is necessary in society today. Their voices are needed in the education system with all the "critical race theory and woke-ism" going on. Their voices are needed in a government where it's spends and spends and keeps on spending. Their voices are needed in entertainment where perversion is the norm of the day. Their voices are needed in the church, the Body of Christ, where much of the church has forgotten the cross, the blood, repentance, sacrifice, sanctification, retribution and denying oneself.

There are some of you who are experiencing things right now that you can't explain, things you don't understand. There has been a stirring inside of you, and you aren't sure what it is, you can't explain it. God has given you power from on high. The Apostle John said that we have an anointing, an unction from the Holy One and that we know all things. (I John 2:20)

The generation of Issachar is important, not because God is not doing anything and we have to think of something for Him to do, but because we must know what are the things that God is presently doing. All of us, according to the Word of God, should not be led by the flesh but by the Spirit of God.

Being part of the Issachar generation will cause you to face opposition.

In 1 Chronicles 12, it tells us that there were those who were equipped for war and joined with David at Hebron. The purpose of these men coming together was to turn the kingdom over to David. These men were well prepared and ready for opposition and resistance. These men of Israel were locking arm-in-arm with David, so that they may establish him king as God had spoken it to be.

These men who came didn't wish they were somewhere else; they adjusted to the times and accomplished what could not be easily attained. The thing that God has purposed will always be resisted by the kingdom of darkness.

Even though we fight from a position of victory, the enemies of God will continue to resist. Advancing the kingdom of God has never been without resistance, Jesus said, **"The kingdom of heaven suffers violence and the violent take it by force."**

Throughout time, every time period of history, in every generation, there have been people who have gotten discouraged and felt the hopelessness due to difficult circumstances. I'm sure they wished they could have lived in another time period. As for you, God wants you to know, YOU ARE HERE FOR SUCH A TIME AS THIS!

We shouldn't allow a future to be created for us by people who have no concept of God or His ways; a society that is bent on doing everything they can to remove the very existence of God from our society and culture. Church listen: don't get discouraged! God always has a people, a remnant that will not bow, retreat, turn back or give up! A remnant, a generation that understands the times and hears from God and knows what to do.

The future doesn't just happen, it's built by the preparation *in the now*, the today. The devil isn't just going to roll over and let you have it. There are some who are trying to secure wealth and pleasures; but you and I, the church must secure and raise a generation, an Issachar Generation.

The future generation cannot be secured and raised by just videos, pizzas, games, or conferences. The future generation must be secured, and raised in the power of a Holy God. This generation must see that it is real, that it's not just talk; it must be demonstrated in our lives!

Jesus said that the gates of hell shall not prevail against His church. Too many think that the church is at the point of just maintaining. If we have no faith in this coming generation, it's because we have either neglected to impart to that generation, or we don't have anything to impart to them. We better get a hold of something that is worth imparting.

Importance of Issachar Generation

The presence of and interaction of an Issachar Generation is crucial in this time. Their presence and their voice is needed. What are they hearing? What are they seeing? Multitudes are in the valley of decision, many are confused: gender-confused, sexually-confused and morally confused.

In the last twenty years, the things that we held as *truths*, have been tossed out of the window. Our morals, our convictions, our choosing right from wrong, honesty, integrity, marriage, men being men, women being women - these truths have all been set aside. We are being told that we have to embrace a new set of morality; a morality where anything goes, everything is permissible. Along with this, we are also being told to use a new language, a language where we have to watch what we say, because we might offend someone.

"They are deeply corrupted, As in the days of Gibeah. He will remember their iniquity; He will punish their sins. I found Israel Like grapes in the wilderness; I saw your fathers As the firstfruits on the fig tree in its first season. But they went to Baal Peor, And separated themselves to that shame; They became an abomination like the thing they loved." (Hosea 9:9-10)

The Prophet Hosea is talking about being given over to filth and shame, and sexual perversion.

Shameful abominations had spread throughout Israel. You might be asking, "What happen at Gibeah?" In Judges Chapter 20, in the city of Benjamin, homosexuals raped the concubine of a visiting priest because they couldn't have the priest himself, they left her to die on the doorstep the next day.

When the rest of Israel heard and found out what had happen there, they came to the tribe of Benjamin saying, "There has to be justice." The nation of Benjamin rose up and said, "No, they have a right to be what they are." Over 25,000 men died to protect Gibeah's homosexual rights. They died not for justice, but for Gibeah's immorality and sexual perversion.

"Just as I saw Ephraim like Tyre, planted in a pleasant place, So Ephraim will bring out his children to the murderer." (Hosea 9:13)

It says that children will be given over to murderers. Children are being killed in our schools, in neighborhoods, theaters, playgrounds and in their homes. Children are being destroyed by drugs, alcohol, gangs, social media and abuse – WE NEED TO UNDERSTAND THE TIMES.

"You have plowed wickedness; You have reaped iniquity. You have eaten the fruit of lies, Because you trusted in your own way, In the multitude of your mighty men. Therefore tumult shall arise among your people..." (Hosea 10:13-14)

There will be tumult and uprisings among the people. There will be riots and disorder. What a sad day when most of the so-called leadership in our nation today, instead of bringing people together, they're doing their best to divide it: divide the races, divide the classes, and divide us over illegal immigration.

"Sow for yourselves righteousness; Reap in mercy; Break up your fallow ground, For it is time to seek the Lord, Till He comes and rains (aiming an arrow) righteousness on you." (Hosea 10:12)

In the midst of the tumult, the riots, sexual perversion, there will be an outpouring of righteousness. It says that God will come and rain righteousness. God will shoot His arrow of righteousness down to create a hunger and thirst in us.

What we should understand is that when God says that He is going to rain down as aiming an arrow, this means that it's not going to hit everybody; it will fall wherever God finds a people who truly hunger and thirst after Jesus.

The Isachar Generation is not coming - it is already here! They're speaking to us what the Lord is doing at this time. They're a mighty generation. They're men and women of valor. They understand the surroundings. They can sense the season.

This Issachar Generation run like mighty men and women. They don't break ranks. They run in the city. They run on the wall. They can't be stopped. They're going to turn the world upside down.

When we look around at all the things that are presently happening in our world and society today, we can get discouraged very easily. What we must know is that God is great and greatly to be praised! God is pouring out His Spirit on all flesh. Remember the word of the Lord that says, **"Where sin abounds so much more grace abounds."**

If you are saying to yourself, "I want to be part of this Isachar Generation!" - then it's time to wake-up, get up and get out!

Chapter 5

The Samson Generation:
A Warfare Generation

"Again the children of Israel did evil in the sight of the Lord, and the Lord delivered them into the hand of the Philistines for forty years. Now there was a certain man from Zorah, of the family of the Danites, whose name was Manoah; and his wife was barren and had no children. And the Angel of the Lord appeared to the woman and said to her, "Indeed now, you are barren and have borne no children, but you shall conceive and bear a son. Now therefore, please be careful not to drink wine or similar drink, and not to eat anything unclean. For behold, you shall conceive and bear a son. And no razor shall come upon his head, for the child shall be a Nazirite to God from the womb; and he shall begin to deliver Israel out of the hand of the Philistines." (Judges 13:1-5)

There are generations that Jesus is raising up in the last days. Each generation has a distinct call, anointing, and function to bring about the awesomeness of God to this world and the church.

What kind of generation will come forth in these last days and bring the church of Jesus Christ into the place of victory? What kind of generation will bring people out of sin, wickedness, and set the captives free?

Pastor Tom Carubba

I believe that a *Samson Generation* will be that kind of generation. Now when I say a *Samson Generation*, I'm making reference to a specific characteristic that this generation possesses.

Birthed in Fire

"So Manoah took the young goat with the grain offering, and offered it upon the rock to the Lord. And He did a wondrous thing while Manoah and his wife looked on it happened as the flame went up toward heaven from the altar — the Angel of the Lord ascended in the flame of the altar! When Manoah and his wife saw this, they fell on their faces to the ground." (Judges 13:19-20)

In Exodus 3:21, it says that the Angel of the Lord appeared to Moses. This was the man God was choosing to be the deliverer and God spoke to him from a flame of fire out of the midst of a burning bush.

The Prophet Jeremiah was told by the Lord that He would make His words in his mouth a fire and the people as wood (Jeremiah 5:20.)

When one of the live coals was taken out of the altar by a seraphim and the coal touched Isaiah's mouth, the angel said, **"Behold, this has touched your lips; You iniquity is taken away, and your sin purged." It was then that Isaiah heard the Lord ask, "Whom shall I send, and who will go for us?"** Isaiah's response was, HERE AM I, SEND ME!

When the fire of the Lord comes upon you, you will be a different person and will never to be the same again. You will be enlisted in the army of the Lord and given His weapons to fight the good fight.

John the Baptist was out in the desert preaching repentance to all who came out to hear him; he was asked if he was the Christ or not. John's answer was that he indeed baptized them with water, but there was One mightier than he, who was coming; He would baptize them with the Holy Spirit and fire. John said that His fan was in His hand and He would clean out the threshing floor, gather the wheat into His barn, but the chaff He would burn with unquenchable fire!

This is not a time to slack off or compromise, the fire of the Lord is coming upon the whole world; the question that we need to ask ourselves is, "Am I ready?"

Jesus is coming, the hour is late. I must ask myself if the fire of the Holy Spirit is upon me. The fire of the Lord burns up that which is not good. The Word of God states that every man's work will be tried by fire to see what kind of work it is!

Generation Of Warfare

The *Samson Generation* will be a generation of warfare. Samson was always fighting, never giving up, always battling the enemy. It states that the Spirit of the Lord began to move upon Samson.

In Judges chapter 14, it says that a young lion roared against Samson and the Spirit of the Lord came mightily upon him. Samson tore the lion to pieces!

There was another time when Samson caught three hundred foxes, tied them together at their tails, then took firebrands between the two tails and let the foxes loose to run through the Philistines field of corn destroying their harvest of the corn.

Needless to say, the Philistines were very upset and wanted to capture Samson and get rid of him. The Philistines went up to Judah and the men of Judah came out to them and asked them why they came up here to fight against us. The answer they gave was that all they wanted was to arrest Samson for what he did to their fields.

It states that three thousand men from Judah went down to the cleft of the rock of Etam and said to Samson, "Do you not know that the Philistines rule over us? What have you done to us?" Samson's response was, "As they did to me, so I have done to them."

The *Samson Generation* will be the generation that will say, "If those speaking lies can stand on a street corner and spew out lies, than I can stand on the same corner and speak the truth."

If the LGBT community can march down Main Street and not be ashamed of their perverted lifestyle, then the Samson generation doesn't have to be behind closed doors; as a matter of fact it should be out there in the highways and byways combating the evil perversion that is destroying the lives of our children.

We all know that the LGBT community have made inroads into society. We have in major cities transvestites in public libraries reading to children during story time. If you're a Christian and stand against them reading stories to little children, much of the response is, "What and why do we have something against them reading to children?" But the *Samson's Generation* question to the LGBT and city councils is, "Why do you feel the need that you have to read to little children?"

Much of the Church will never ask that question; and the reason why they don't and won't, is because they don't want to be labeled homophobic, haters, or racist. I believe the real reason they wouldn't ask is because they have allowed fear to take root in their lives.

When you continue reading in Judges Chapter 15, the men of Judah tell Samson that they won't kill him, but what they will do is tie him up and deliver him to the Philistines. The *Samson Generation* is a generation of warfare; it's a generation of speaking the truth no matter who agrees with it or not.

The sad thing is that the church that has given itself over to being politically correct and not wanting to offend anyone. You see, this is the church that will give the *Samson Generation* over to a perverted society. The *lukewarm* church is selling out the *Samson Generation*!

Remember the *Samson Generation* is part of God's church, they are brothers and sisters in Christ; but the modern Church does not want to cause any waves. They want the *Samson Generation* to *lighten up* and quit causing problems, until finally, they end up abandoniong the *Samson Generation*.

God had a different plan. When Samson came to Lehi, the Philistines came towards Samson shouting against him. Then the Spirit of the Lord came mightily upon Samson and the robes that had him tied up were broken and Samson found a jawbone of a donkey and killed a thousand men with it.

In Judges 16, we see Samson waiting until midnight came and then he took the doors of the gate of the city along with the two posts; he then put them on his shoulders and carried them up to the top of the hill; this is a type and symbol of the gates of hell shall not prevailing against the church of Jesus Christ.

What we have to understand is that gates are a defense. Too much of the church has bought into the mindset that says, let us *"circle the wagons and hang on until Jesus comes."* Too many times, we as Christians have been attacked, and we want to be on the defense when according to what Jesus said, we are to be on the attack.

If gates are a defense and the gates of hell cannot prevail against us, then we have to be the ones attacking. Think about this: just about in every city there is an area where the church has allowed the devil to have his way. This shouldn't be. The Body of Christ should not give any ground to the enemy; we are to take dominion of the land! The *Samson Generation* knows this principle well, and that's why they're warring against evil.

Know this, God will bring us into battle, into warfare. Matthew 4:1 states that after Christ was baptized, He was led by the Spirit of God into the wilderness to be tempted of the devil. Notice what it says: it was the Spirit of God that led Jesus into the wilderness to be tempted, to do battle, to do warfare, to be victorious.

The Devil Will Try to Find the Samson's Generation Weakness.

Remember how Samson carried at midnight the doors of the gate of the city to the top of the hill - but why was Samson there in the city of Gaza? Samson had a weakness and that weakness was women. Samson was there in the city because he was with a harlot.

I remember hearing my pastor saying, *It is good to know your strengths; but it's crucial to know your weaknesses*. Even Superman had a weakness that he couldn't handle, it was kryptonite. We know from the beginning of Samson's adulthood that his weakness was women. Time and time again he allowed himself to get tangled up in lust. Somewhere along the way someone who had been looking, observing and studying Samson's movements; and in his life it was concluded that his weakness was women.

The Philistines found a woman named Delilah. The lords of the Philistines went to Delilah and promised to give her a hundred pieces of silver; all she would have to do is find out where Samson's great strength was, and how they can overpower and bind him.

Delilah goes to Samson the first time and says to him, **"Tell me where does your great strength come from?" And Samson said to her, "If they bind me with seven fresh bowstrings, not yet dried, then I shall become weak, and be like any other man."** (Judges 16:7)

Delilah binds Samson and calls the Philistines, but Samson breaks free and escapes.

After this Samson goes back to Delilah again, and she tells Samson that he has mocked her and told her lies about his strength. She asks Samson again how he could be bound. Then Samson said that if they bind him with new ropes that were never used, then he would become weak. So what does Delilah do, she binds him with seven new ropes and calls the Philistines again, but Samson again broke the ropes off and escaped.

Samson comes back a third time, and Delilah criticizes Samson saying that again he lied to her and made her look foolish. So Samson tells her this time that if she weaved the seven locks of his head, he would become weak as any other man.

Notice that Samson is getting closer and closer to revealing what gives him his strength. Delilah takes it a step further and not only does she weave his hair, but she pins it to the headboard. She calls for the Philistines to come and Samson wakes up and escapes with the headboard pinned to him.

Once again, Samson returns back to Delilah. This is the fourth time. You would think that after two times and definitely after three times, he would have realize that this woman is not good for him. You see, not only does Samson have a weakness, but he is hooked on the weakness; he can't shake it off. Delilah asks Samson that, how he can say he loves her, when he has mocked her three times and not told her the truth.

It says that daily she pressed him until Samson finally gave in and told her all his heart. The secret was out, Samson told her that a razor has never come upon his head, and that that was the secret of his strength.

We need to ask ourselves some deep questions. You see, it is easy to look at Samson and say to ourselves, "I would never do that!" Let's be honest, where is our own weakness? Is it pride in what we have accomplished? Is it jealousy? Is it in pursuing popularity? Do I give into peer pressure? Or is there envy in my heart? What about relationships - do they take priority over Biblical principles? Do I make excuses for certain lifestyles? We have to be honest with ourselves.

Delilah sees that Samson has held nothing back from her; his secret has been exposed and now she will use it against him. Delilah causes Samson to fall asleep in her lap, then calls for someone to come and shave his seven locks from his head. After Samson's head is shaved, Delilah starts to "afflict," torment, and hurt him.

Samson falls asleep in the devil's lap. He's lying there as comfortable as can be, and doesn't even know what's about to happen to him. If Samson represents the church, the Body of Christ, then we have to realize that many Christians today have fallen asleep and are being deceived by secular humanism and politically-correct crowds. Many are allowing these crowds to dictate to them what is normal and what can be said.

It's the Word of God, God Himself, that says what is normal! In Romans 12, the Apostle Paul states, **"I beseech you therefore, brethren,**

by the mercies of God, that you present your bodies a living sacrifice, holy, acceptable to God, which is your reasonable (rational, logical) service. And do not be conformed to this world, but be transformed by the renewing of your mind, that you may prove what is that good and acceptable and perfect will of God."

There will be those who won't realize that the Spirit of God has left them. Delilah has Samson's head shaved, his strength is now gone from him, and she cries out, "The Philistines are here!" Samson not knowing that the Spirit of God has departed, awakes out of his sleep and says to himself, **"I will go out as I have done before and take care of the problem, but didn't know that the Lord had departed from him."**

Samson is captured and the Philistines put out his eyes; they took him down to Gaza, bound him and put him to grind in the prison house. The first thing that happened to Samson was that he lost his sight, he lost his vision. Without vision you don't know where you are going; you will have to be led. What we have to ask ourselves is, "Who is leading us? Who is leading the church?"

The majority of the church world has lost its vision; they have lost their vision to see people saved and be set free. Many have lost their burden and desire to see people come to Jesus; others have lost the desire to proclaim that Jesus is coming back and are you ready for Him?

Too much of the Body of Christ is concerned with their own self and their own happiness that they hardly tell anyone what Jesus can do for them if they turn to Him. Only Jesus can forgive them, only He can give them hope and bring them out of a pit of despair, discouragement, and torment.

Jesus's commanded His disciples, and it's the same command that you and I still have today. That command is to GO INTO ALL THE WORLD AND PREACH THE GOSPEL. Not the gospel of self, not the gospel of inclusion, not the gospel of hyper-grace, but the true Gospel of Jesus Christ. That Jesus Christ came into the world to save sinners; to give us not just life, but life abundantly; to give us authority and to tread upon serpents and scorpions and to have all power over the enemy.

The second thing that happened to Samson after his eyes were taken out and became blind, was that he was put at the mill to grind. Here we find Samson, the representation of the church, just going around in circles day after day and hour after hour. In another words, Samson (represents the church,) did the same thing over and over - it was just routine, he was only going through the motions.

Many Christians are going through the motions every week. It's Sunday, so we go to the church building; we sing our songs, maybe lift our hands, we stand, we sit and we endure a sermonette and then go home. Week after week, month after month and year after year, we just go through the motions. Many ask, "Where is the power and where is the healing; where is the deliverance that sets people free from addiction of sin?

Samson Becomes An Laughing Stock

In Judges 16, it says that the lords of the Philistines came together to offer a great sacrifice unto Dagon their god. The reason why they came together was to rejoice and celebrate. Why the celebration? Well, they believed their god delivered Samson into their hands. As time went on at the celebration they decided to bring Samson out of the prison house so that they could make fun of him, to laugh at him.

Over the years, too much of the church has become a laughing stock to the world. The world looks at the church and laughs. Is it any wonder why the world laughs: when they hear of the money scandals, the sex scandals, the foolishness of how people carry on claiming this and declaring that, and it (prophecies) that never comes to pass; not to mention all the tearing down and pulling apart of each other. The world hears a lot of talk, but very little action.

Samson Generation Will Be Put In Position

When they brought Samson out and after they mocked and ridiculed him, Samson asked a young boy that was by him if he would lead him by the hand between the two pillars, so that he could lean on them.

Here's the good news of the *Samson Generation*: Samson (the church) is led by a young boy to the place, to the position where he can make a difference and cause the most damaged to the kingdom of the enemy.

Can God count on you to be the generation that can be brought into the right position; and when brought to this position, and just like with Samson, attain a greater victory at the end than at the beginning? It says of Samson that he destroyed more enemies at the end of his life then he did throughout his whole life.

The Word of God says that the glory of the latter house *shall be*, not maybe, not hopefully, but it will be greater than that of the former house!

WE HAVEN'T SEEN ANYTHING YET!!!!

Where sin abounds, so much more does grace abound. The church of Jesus Christ will go out in a blaze of glory. Elijah went out in a chariot of fire.

Do you want to be part of this generation? Then declare that you will be that generation, a *Samson Generation!* It is a generation that will be true to the calling that God has given it. It's a call that will tread upon serpents and scorpions and nothing shall by any means harm it.

Here's what you must know: Greater works shall you do, because Jesus has anointed you for such a time as this!

Chapter 6

The Elijah Generation:
Restoration Generation

"Behold, I will send you Elijah the prophet Before the coming of the great and dreadful day of the Lord. And he will turn The hearts of the fathers to the children, And the hearts of the children to their fathers, Lest I come and strike the earth with a curse." (Malachi 4:5, 6)

Like we have stated before in previous chapters, a generation is a time period. Usually a generation goes like this, grandfather, father, then son or grand-parents, parents, then children.

The Word of Lord tells us that before Jesus returns, there will be an *Elijah Generation* (spirit of Elijah, the voice of one crying,) that will come forth with a message that will cause the fathers hearts to be returned to the children and that the heart of the children will return to their fathers. This is something both in the natural and the spiritual.

The Word of God says, **"Though you have ten thousand instructors in Christ, yet you don't have many fathers."** We need fathers in and of the faith that have stood the test of time, that have set the example as to how to follow Jesus.

This *Elijah Generation* will be used by God to turn many to righteousness and making ready a people prepared also to be used by the Lord. **Transfigured!**

"Now after six days Jesus took Peter, James, and John his brother, led them up on a high mountain by themselves; and He was transfigured before them. His face shone like the sun, and His clothes became as white as the light. And behold, Moses and Elijah appeared to them, talking with Him. Then Peter answered and said to Jesus, "Lord, it is good for us to be here; if You wish, let us make here three tabernacles: one for You, one for Moses, and one for Elijah." (Matthew 17:1-4)

The Word of God says that Jesus was instantaneously transformed right before Peter, James and John eyes. Jesus' face shone like the sun, and His clothes became as white as the light.

Imagine for a moment, what an experience this was for Peter, James and John? When they heard the voice of God saying, **"This is My beloved Son whom I am well pleased, listen to Him,"** they fell on their faces as many of us would have, in fear and in awe. In that moment, the same Moses who led the Israelites out of Egypt, and the same Elijah who prayed down fire from heaven, were standing there with Jesus in a transfigured (changed) state.

When Peter, James and John were making their way back down from the mountain where the other disciples were, they asked Jesus a question – **"Why then do the scribes say that Elijah must come first?"** (Matthew 17:10)

Jesus responds and says, **"Indeed Elijah is coming first and will restore all things, but I say to you that Elijah has already come and they did not know him, but they did not whatever they wished. Likewise the Son of Man is also about to suffer at their hands."** It says that after Jesus spoke these words that the disciples understood that Jesus was speaking to them about John the Baptist."** (Matthew 17:11-13)

The disciples believed that John was a prophet who had the touch of God on his life; but now the disciples understood that John had come in the spirit of Elijah.

"And he will turn many of the children of Israel to the Lord their God. He will also go before Him in the spirit and power of Elijah, 'to turn the hearts of the fathers to the children,' and the disobedient to the wisdom of the just, to make ready a people prepared (equipped) for the Lord." (Luke 1:16-17)

John would be anointed as Elijah was; he would preach a message of repentance that would cause the people to return to the Lord and to worship Him in truth.

You can watch Christian television and listen to Christian radio, and hardly ever hear anyone, or hear a message on the subject of repentance. You can't make a people ready and prepared for the Lord, unless they know that they have to repent of their sins and be reconciled back to God.

Calling a Nation to Return

It was during one of the times of deep spiritual darkness in Israel's history, that the Holy Spirit empowered Elijah to call the nation to repentance and back to the Lord. We are in a dark spiritual time in our nation and in the Church today.

With drugs, addictions, same sex marriage, gender confusion, sin and perversion out in the open on our nation's main streets - one has to wonder: *Where are the praying Christians? Where are the voices calling the nation and the church back to repentance? Where are the messages that preach: "Turn your back on sin and pursue righteousness!"*

In 1 Kings 18, the Prophet Elijah is calling out the prophets of Baal who had introduced a false god to Israel; they had caused the Israelites to follow a self-seeking and self-gratifying lifestyle.

Due to these false prophets, there was a downward spiral in Israel's spirituality. The nation of Israel became completely compromised, causing false prophets to increase by numbers in the land.

There were two altars built. One was the altar of Baal where four hundred and fifty false prophets were worshiping. These prophets had the support of Jezebel, King Ahab's wife; and were eating at her table in the palace. These prophets had influence in political matters that affected the nation of Israel.

This is exactly what is happening in our nation and culture today.

There's now a generation of false prophets in our government and in the Body of Christ who operate out of lust and greed.

When these things happen, they will always cause harm to the people of that nation. All you have to do is look around: the poor go hungry, the fatherless are not cared for, the widows aren't visited in their grief. This happens because of a selfish pursuit where people only want to know what's in it for them.

The other altar that was built, was built by Elijah. This altar represented the true worship of the One True God. Elijah built the right altar. His motive was to turn the hearts of the people from a false religion to having a right relationship with the true God.

When things are done right, the fire of God falls. The fire of the Lord came down, burned up the sacrifice, the wood, the stones and the soil, and also licked up the water in the trench. When the people saw this, they fell prostrate and cried out, **"The Lord, He is God. The Lord, He is God."**

The *Elijah Generation* is a ministry; it is a voice pointing people to Jesus, the only Way, the only Truth and the only Life!

Calling to Repentance

The calling to repentance is the calling that John the Baptist had when he was baptizing men and women in the River Jordan; he was calling them to repentance.

John was a man who didn't care what society thought of him. He lived and ministered without being affected by the influences around him. His main concern was for men and women to go in the right direction towards Jesus. John pointed people to Jesus declaring Jesus to be the Lamb of God who takes away the sins of the world. John was building the Kingdom of God, not establishing an empire for himself.

Those who heard John's message repented and were baptized, then were told to follow Jesus. When the religious leaders asked John who he was, he didn't focus on himself or his ministry, John's reply was, "Im not even worthy to untie the shoelaces of Jesus!"

John the Baptist was simply a voice for God. John's message that he communicated to men and women was that there is a Messiah (Jesus,) who needs to be revered and a hell to be shunned and a heaven to be gained.

This is the voice that is need today! The voice of an *Elijah Generation*; one that is not ashamed of Jesus no matter where they are. They can be in their home, the workplace, with family, or at school. They will be a voice that will not be silent when people are dying in their sins.

Now is the time for us to receive the power of God so that we may do whatever He commands us to do; that we may go wherever He sends us and speak what He has tells us to speak; even if it doesn't make sense to the natural mind.

Calling to Restoration

The Prophet Elijah caused Israel to return to true worship. John the Baptist called the people to repentance.

When Jesus was coming down from the mountain He spoke these words, in Matthew 17:11: **"Indeed, Elijah is coming first and will restore all things."** Restore means to bring back to its former condition; to restore health and soundness, to reform something, to bring back a lost dominion and authority.

The same power of the Holy Spirit that was given to Elijah and to John, was demonstrated once again on the Day of Pentecost in the lives of those in the upper room.

In the upper room there were 120 people who were fearful, but were praying and waiting on God like they were told to do. They were ordinary everyday people. Most were by that standards of the day, uneducated and unlearned.

All of a sudden, the Holy Spirit descended on them and empowered them with strength and authority to speak a message that would restore the hearts of the people back to God. This power of God, gave them the ability to go places they could have never gone in their own strength.

When these 120 disciples were baptized with the Holy Spirit, faith exploded in their hearts. The next thing we know, is that they're out in the streets publicly and unashamedly, proclaiming that Jesus Christ had risen from the dead. The people heard and responded by asking, **"What must I do to be saved?"** On that day, 3,000 people came to Jesus. This is the *Elijah Generation* in action!

Everyone that has called upon the name of the Lord can have this same power. We can be an *Elijah Generation* in a world that is on the brink of disaster. We can call men and women to return to the true worship of God.

If this is your desire, ask the Lord for His heart for the lost. Ask to see as Jesus sees; ask Him for the authority to establish you as a witness of His power, His grace, His mercy in your home, at your workplace, at your school, and in the community you live in.

If the 120 in the Upper Room could change the known world of their day by the power of the Holy Spirit, how much more can we change and influence our world by this same power? Now, we won't change anything, if we ourselves aren't changed.

Have we changed our ways and our mindsets? Have we repented of our sins? Are we walking in the newness of the life of Jesus Christ?

Prayer: *"Jesus fill me, empower me, and use me. Take me where I could never go. Make me to become what I could never become in mine own strength; and anoint the words You put in my heart to speak."* Amen.

Chapter 7

The Josiah Generation: Reviving A Generation

What is revival? There are many places that claim that revival is where they are at; or at least where Christian magazines say that revival is happening.

There are those who think that revival is numbers; if there's a lot of people it must be God. But in all honesty, what brings genuine revival? Revival is a sovereign move of God; but has a human element to it. In saying this, God still needs a people to bring about revival.

When Evan Roberts of the Welsh revival was asked if God could send another revival, he said only if God could find a person with a right heart.

A true revival will take you pass the shouting, the thrills, the rolling, the bucking, the shaking and the emotions. A true revival causes changes in our life; it will change the direction we were going, and gives us fresh eyes and ears to see and hear the cries of the people.

A true revival will *wreck* our life and then give us a new life in Jesus Christ; a life to go into the highways and byways and tell the people, "Jesus is coming, are you ready?"

"Josiah was eight years old when he began to reign, and he reigned

thirty and one years in Jerusalem. And his mother's name was Jedidah, the daughter of Adaiah of Boscath. And he did that which was right in the sight of the Lord, and walked in all the way of David his father, and turned not aside to the right hand or to the left." (2 Kings 22: 1-2)

"And the king sent, and they gathered unto him all the elders of Judah and of Jerusalem. And the king went up into the house of the Lord, and all the men of Judah and all the inhabitants of Jerusalem with him, and the priests, and the prophets, and all the people, both small and great: and he read in their ears all the words of the book of the covenant which was found in the house of the Lord.And the king stood by a pillar, and made a covenant before the Lord, to walk after the Lord, and to keep his commandments and his testimonies and his statutes with all their heart and all their soul, to perform the words of this covenant that were written in this book. And all the people stood to the covenant." (2 Kings 23:1-3)

"And like unto him was there no king before him, that turned to the Lord with all his heart, and with all his soul, and with all his might, according to all the law of Moses; neither after him arose there any like him." (2 Kings 23:25)

Importance of God's Word In Revival

It's the Word of God that changes people's lives. In 2 Kings 22, Hilkiah the high priest found the book of the law, he gave it to Shaphan the scribe and Shaphan read it. Shaphan went to King Josiah and when he heard the words of the book, Josiah rent his clothes.

The Word of God brought understanding and conviction to King Josiah. **Note:** At the age of sixteen years old, Josiah broke down the graven images and destroyed the altars in the high places that many in the kingdom were worshipping.

The history of Josiah, was that at eight years old, he started to reign in Jerusalem. His reign would be for thirty years. In the Book of Chronicles chapter 34, it states that Josiah did that which was right in the sight of the Lord; he walked in the ways of his father King David, and didn't turn to the right hand and neither to the left hand.

It was in the eighth year of his reign that he began to seek the God of David his father, and it was in the twelfth year of his reign, that he began to purge Judah and Jerusalem from the high places, the groves and the carved and molten images.

Why did Josiah start to do these things? It was the Word of God that gave Josiah the reason for being! It says in 2 Kings 13, that a man of God, out of Judah, cried against the altar and his cry was, **"O altar, altar, this is what the Lord says: "Behold a child shall be born unto the house of David, Josiah by name and upon him shall destroy the priest who burn incense upon the high altars."**

Through this prophecy and the reading of it, Josiah found his destiny, his future, and his purpose. It tells us that we have to open the Bible, the Word of God, and read it and find out what it says, not what we think it says.

The Word of God has a prophecy concerning us. In Acts chapter 2, verse 17, it says, **"And it shall come to pass in the last days, says God, That I will pour out of My Spirit on all flesh; Your sons and your daughters shall prophesy, Your young men shall see visions, Your old men shall dream dreams."**

In Psalms 102 verse 18, the Psalmist says concerning a prophecy that there will be a generation that will come, a people yet to be created may praise the Lord.

Jesus Himself said, **"But the hour is coming, and now is, when the true worshipers will worship the Father in spirit and truth; for the Father is seeking such to worship Him."** Jesus then goes on to say that, **"...he who believes in Him, the works that He does will we also be able to do, and not only the works He did, but greater works than those he will do because He goes to the Father."** (John 14:12)

Spirit Of God Sought

"Go, inquire of the Lord for me, for the people and for all Judah, concerning the words of this book that has been found; for great is the wrath of the Lord that is aroused against us, because our fathers have not obeyed the words of this book, to do according to all that is written concerning us." So Hilkiah the priest, Ahikam, Achbor, Shaphan, and Asaiah went to Huldah the prophetess, the wife of Shallum the son of Tikvah, the son of Harhas, keeper of the wardrobe. (She dwelt in Jerusalem in the Second Quarter.) And they spoke with her. Then she said to them, "Thus says the Lord God of Israel, 'Tell the man who sent you to Me, "Thus says the Lord: 'Behold, I will bring calamity on this place and on its inhabitants — all the words of the book which the king of Judah has read because they have forsaken Me and burned incense to other gods, that they might provoke Me to anger with all the works of their hands. Therefore My wrath shall be aroused against this place and shall not be quenched.'"' But as for the king of Judah, who sent you to inquire of the Lord, in this manner you shall speak to him, 'Thus says the Lord God of Israel: "Concerning the words which you have heard because your heart was tender, and you humbled yourself before the Lord when you heard what I spoke against this place and against its inhabitants, that they would become a desolation and a curse, and you tore your clothes and wept before Me, I also have heard you," says the Lord. Surely, therefore, I will gather you to your fathers, and you shall be gathered to your grave in peace; and your eyes shall not see all the calamity which I will bring on this place.'"' So they brought back word to the king."** (2 Kings 22:13-20)

The Spirit of God brings confirmation, assurance and direction. Confirmation is something that proves; assurance is confidence, certainty, direction, order, or command. You can go to the Word of God and get these things for your life.

A Right Heart Brings Revival

Heart attitude is important. The Word of God tells us to keep our hearts with all diligence, because out of the heart springs the issues, the boundaries of life. In Proverbs, it tells us that as we think in our heart, so are we. Paul wrote to the Church in Rome and said to them, **"for with the heart one believes unto righteousness."**

We can see just from these verses that the heart of man plays an important part in bringing revival. God looks on the heart of man. The question we have to ask ourselves is, "What does God see?"

What Kind Of Heart Did Josiah Have?

The first thing we know about Josiah, is that he had a heart that was right or in good standing with God. A right heart is straight and just. It says in 2 Kings chapter 22, that Josiah did what was right in the sight of the Lord and walked in all the ways of his father David; he didn't turn to the right or to the left.

God always looks on the heart. What is my heart? What is my reason? What do I want and why do I want it? Why do I want revival? Why does a Church want revival? Is it for numbers? Is it for finances? Is it for fame and popularity? Do I want revival because I want God's manifested glory and majesty to bring people to repentance and salvation? The heart will reveal what the true reason is!

The second thing that Josiah had, was a *repented* heart. It states that when Josiah heard the words of the Book of the Law, he tore his clothes. Tearing of the clothes is an outward sign of repentance. Repentance is a 180 degree turn around. Repentance causes you to think differently.

The Apostle Paul said that the things he used to do, he doesn't do them anymore; in in the same manner, the things he didn't do, now he does! The evidence of a repentant heart is a changed lifestyle. It's living differently than you lived before and people taking notice of the change or the transformation.

The third thing Josiah had was a tender heart. This type of tender heart made him to humble himself before the Lord. Josiah's heart was tender; it was soften. He received God's Word and trembled at it. Not only trembled at it, but yielded himself to it. He was grieved over the dishonor that was done to God by the sins of his fathers and of the people.

He also feared the judgments of God and wanted to turn God's judgment away. Can God still move on your heart or has it become hard with walls around it? Can you be moved with compassion? Do you care about people and their souls?

The fourth thing Josiah had, was a *committed* heart. A *committed* heart is a heart that turns to the Lord wholeheartedly; with all its strength. What Josiah set out to do, he did; and no one swayed him. We can say he went for broke and held nothing back. We are to love the Lord with everything that is in us. It's like the old song we use to sing in our Churches, "In Him we live, and move and have our being."

"Trust in the Lord with all your heart, And lean not on your own understanding." (Proverbs 3:5)

Can we say, "I'm committed to the call of God, the work of God, the house of God and the ministry of God, that He has given me?" Revival will come - ready or not. We can prepare and be ready for it. We know how revival comes.

"If My people who are called by My name will humble themselves, and pray and seek My face, and turn from their wicked ways, then I will hear from heaven, and will forgive their sin and heal their land." (2 Chronicles 7:14)

What kind of heart is God looking for? A heart that is right, repented, tender and committed? Now the real question to ask yourself is, "Do we have this kind of heart?" God has great plans for us and His Church.

I do believe that greater works shall we do - because Jesus goes to the Father; and Jesus will send the Comforter who will lead us into all truth!

Chapter 8

The Ezra Generation:
Awakening a Generation

The Ezra Generation will be the generation to call a nation and people to repentance and lead the way for people to come back into right covenant with God.

"Now all the people gathered together as one man in the open square that was in front of the Water Gate; and they told Ezra the scribe to bring the Book of the Law of Moses, which the Lord had commanded Israel. So Ezra the priest brought the Law before the assembly of men and women and all who could hear with understanding on the first day of the seventh month. Then he read from it in the open square that was in front of the Water Gate from morning until midday, before the men and women and those who could understand; and he ears of all the people were attentive to the Book of the Law." (Nehemiah 8:1-3)

God chose Ezra to be an instrument of good to the nation Israel; that he might bring honor back in the priesthood. Here is Ezra standing, delivering the Word of the Lord in front of the "Water Gate" (each gate represents a ministry- the water gate represents the ministry of the Word of God).

Ezra was a man of great learning who knew the writings in the Law of

Moses. This man didn't only know the words in the Law, but he knew the meaning of them. Ezra, because of his knowledge of the Scriptures, set himself to teach the statutes and judgments of that law. He prepared his heart before the Lord.

Who Was Ezra?

Ezra was one of the main leaders that left Babylon, along with Nehemiah to rebuild Jerusalem. At this particular time in history, Jerusalem was in ruins.

During this time God didn't just use one man to bring an awakening to the nation of Israel. God raised up *restorers* of the walls, repairers of the breach; God also raised up interceding prophets. Many builders who were willing to work night and day had been raised up for the building.

"If you faint in the day of adversity, day of distress and anguish, then your strength is weak." (Proverbs 24:10)

God raised up people who were touched by the Spirit of God that would come together to cooperate with His plans and purposes at this specific time in history.

In Nehemiah chapter 2, King Artaxerxes gave permission and provision to Nehemiah. It was Nehemiah who would lead the restoration of Jerusalem's wall.

Now, in Ezra chapter 5, Haggai and Zechariah prophesied to the builders who were restoring the temple.

Ezra's responsibility and his purpose was to bring a spiritual revival to God's people by restoring a reverent fear of the Law (Word) of God; and also, a heartfelt worship for the One true and living God, the God who had so many times before delivered them from bondage.

What did Ezra do? Ezra taught the people of God the Word of God. Ezra was determined to teach the Israelites who have been carried away into Babylonian captivity, the Word of God. Ezra, like Nehemiah, also rose up in the reign of Artaxerxes. The Bible describes Ezra as **"a skilled scribe in the Law of Moses, which the Lord God of Israel gave."** (Ezra 7:6)

"For Ezra had prepared his heart to seek the Law of the Lord, and to do it, and to teach statutes and ordinances in Israel." (Ezra 7:10)

When Ezra arrived in Jerusalem, he readily went to work on his assignment; therefore, he prepared (fashioned, make provision) his heart to seek the Lord. When the time came for the walls and the temple to be rebuilt, the family leaders and temple servants, started returning to Jerusalem.

"When these things were done, the leaders came to me, saying, "The people of Israel and the priests and the Levites have not separated themselves from the peoples of the lands, with respect to the abominations of the Canaanites, the Hittites, the Perizzites, the

Jebusites, the Ammonites, the Moabites, the Egyptians, and the Amorites." (Ezra 9:1)

"So when I heard this thing, I tore my garment and my robe, and plucked out some of the hair of my head and beard, and sat down astonished. Then everyone who trembled at the words of the God of Israel assembled to me, because of the transgression of those who had been carried away captive, and I sat astonished until the evening sacrifice." (Ezra 9:3-4)

Call To Repentance

The Ezra Generation will be a generation of men and women who will call a people, a nation back to repentance and to establish a re-covenant with the Lord.

During the evening sacrifice, Ezra rose up with his clothes and robe torn, he knelt on his knees and stretched out his hands in prayer to God and started leading the nation in repentance. **"And I said: "O my God, I am too ashamed and humiliated to lift up my face to You, my God; for our iniquities have risen higher than our heads, and our guilt has grown up to the heavens. Since the days of our fathers to this day we have been very guilty, and for our iniquities we, our kings, and our priests have been delivered into the hand of the kings of the lands, to the sword, to captivity, to plunder, and to humiliation, as it is this day."** (Ezra 9:6-7)

While Ezra was praying (chapter 10), confessing, weeping, and bowing down before the House of the Lord - a group of men, women, and children came to him weeping. Shechaniah said to Ezra, saying, **"We have trespassed against the Lord and have taken pagan wives from the people of the land, but I realize that there is hope in spite of doing this."** Ezra goes on and in essence says, "Let us make a covenant with God to put away all these wives."

Believing For An Awakening

The Israelites confessed their sins, repented, and immediately starting making the wrong things right. What is really happening here is exactly what it says in 2 Chron. 7:14 – **"If My people who are called by My name shall humble themselves, pray, seek My face and turn from their wicked ways, I WILL HEAL THEIR LAND."**

Here are multitudes of God's people who are believing God for another great awakening. They're praying, fasting, declaring, proclaiming and believing. God said He would pour out His Spirit in the last days on all flesh. God said that the glory of the latter house will be greater than the former house.

Can you imagine with me what would happen if tomorrow morning, when you turned on the television, the radio or the internet, you heard Joel Osteen, Andy Stanley, Joyce Meyer, Ed Young Jr., Ken Copeland, Pat Robertson, Matt Crouch, T. D. Jakes and other high profile leaders in the Christian circle make this kind of statement … "The following message is uncharacteristic of our normal broadcast – BUT we are not living in normal times – we can't keep pretending God's judgments aren't real – we can't keep continuing to go on the way we're going on – God has given us just 8 words to share with you – 40 more days and America will be destroyed – BUT there is still hope if we believe that God will have mercy on us if we humbly ourselves and turn back to Him."

Many don't realize that one of the greatest *awakenings* in the history of the world took place when just one man, an obedient servant of God, spoke those very same words to the city of Nineveh. The people of the city were shaken by the severity of the message, that they turned from their sinful ways and returned back to God and God didn't destroy their city. (Jonah 3)

You and I, as Christians, as disciples of Jesus Christ, can't settle any longer for "status quo" religion with neatly packaged, sanitized, inspirational programs and services, while turning our backs and ignoring the epidemic of Christians being persecuted all over the world and our Western civilization crumbling around us.

In Nehemiah, chapter 8, it tells more of the story: Ezra reads the Book of the Law of Moses to all the peoplel then Ezra blessed the Lord as the great God. All that were there responded saying, "Amen, Amen." The people lifted up their hands and they bowed their heads, they worshipped the Lord with their faces to the ground.

Ezra then told the people, **"Go your way, eat the fat and drink the sweet, send portions to those whom nothing is prepared, for this day is holy to the Lord, the joy of the Lord is your strength."** Jerusalem, God's city was restored. America can be restored. The church can be restored. It might look like there is disaster; BUT because of God and His mercy, IT'S NOT TOO LATE to turn a nation around, to turn the Body of Christ, His church around; we need another great awakening!

Thank God that there are multitudes of people, young and old, male and female, that are waking up, rising up, and realizing that the way many have been going - isn't making any sense, and they're saying, "NO MORE!" They realize that we, the CHURCH, the true church, is losing sight of who and what it *really* is and who it is we represent! Thank God that this is changing as men and women take their places and their authority in Jesus!

The *Ezra Generation* is waking up; a generation of sleeping giants that God will be using in the last days as He pours His Spirit upon them.

Chapter 9

An Opportunity Comes to Another Generation!

"Every commandment which I command you today you must be careful to observe, that you may live and multiply, and go in and possess the land of which the Lord swore to your fathers. And you shall remember that the Lord your God led you all the way these forty years in the wilderness, to humble you and test you, to know what was in your heart, whether you would keep His commandments or not. So He humbled you, allowed you to hunger, and fed you with manna which you did not know nor did your fathers know, that He might make you know that man shall not live by bread alone; but man lives by every word that proceeds from the mouth of the Lord. Your garments did not wear out on you, nor did your foot swell these forty years. You should know in your heart that as a man chastens his son, so the Lord your God chastens you. "Therefore you shall keep the commandments of the Lord your God, to walk in His ways and to fear Him. For the Lord your God is bringing you into a good land, a land of brooks of water, of fountains and springs, that flow out of valleys and hills; a land of wheat and barley, of vines and fig trees and pomegranates, a land of olive oil and honey; a land in which you will eat bread without scarcity, in which you will lack nothing; a land whose stones are iron and out of whose hills you can dig copper. When you have eaten and are full, then you shall bless the Lord

your God for the good land which He has given you." (Deuteronomy 8:1-10)

The nation of Israel, the people of God, are at a point in history where forty years before, the generation that came before them and stood at the same borders of promise. It was here where faith was required of them to be able to enter and possess the land.

Faith *Versus* Natural Reasoning

In Numbers chapter 13, Moses sends out twelve spies to search out the land and to see if it was all God said it was. After spying the Promised Land for forty days, ten of the men who came back brought an *evil report*; this caused the people's hearts to turn away from what God had promised them.

An *evil report* means, *defaming and slandering what God had promised.* Two of the spies, *Joshua and Caleb,* reported back also; except their report was a report of faith.

No matter what kind of obstacle they saw; in their hearts, Joshua and Caleb, knew that the promises of God superseded what they saw with their natural eyes; yes, *"It's true, the walls are high and giants occupy the place that is supposed to be ours; but we can go in and take it; God will be faithful to give us what He promised!"*

The ten that came back with an evil report, made a choice; they chose human intellect and reasoning over faith. They brought back an accurate report; yes, they went into the land and brought back real proof of how good is the land; but still God called their report and "evil" report!

In Hebrews chapter 11 and verse 6, the Apostle Paul states, **"But without faith it is impossible to please Him, for he who comes to God must believe that He is, and that He is a Rewarder of those who diligently seek Him."** When Paul spoke to the Church in Rome he said, **"Whatever is not of faith, is sin."** What Paul is saying is that whatever is not of faith is deficient and lacks.

Now understand, we're not saying to throw out or abandon reasoning; but reason has to bring us to faith. Reason can't bring us to seeing what we're seeing with our natural eyes, and then concluding that God is not powerful enough to fulfill His promises in His Word.

Many today will say that the walls were too high; or that evil is too great; or the power of darkness is well entrenched, and we are powerless to move against it - we're not able to do what God is saying. Those are the ones who look into the Word of God and come out with reason responses, instead of faith responses. Humanist reasoning, brings death and despair! That's what it brought to that unbelieving generation in the wilderness; forty years of dying hopes and forty years of decay!

There Comes A Season

"Say to them, 'As I live,' says the Lord, 'just as you have spoken in My hearing, so I will do to you: The carcasses of you who have

An Opportunity Comes to Another Generation!

complained against Me shall fall in this wilderness, all of you who were numbered, according to your entire number, from twenty years old and above. Except for Caleb the son of Jephunneh and Joshua the son of Nun, you shall by no means enter the land which I swore I would make you dwell in. But your little ones, whom you said would be victims, I will bring in, and they shall know the land which you have despised. But as for you, your carcasses shall fall in this wilderness." (Numbers 14:28-32)

The church, that is you and me; we are living in a time and a season in our generation where in the Body of Christ and in our country, many have abandoned their faith due to their human reasoning.

We are presently living in a time where in the church, our faith has been turned into reasoning. Strategies are now being developed, the *how to's* of living a godly life are being developed, the *how to's* of succeeding in life; and countless other *how to's* are now out there!

We can't abandon faith in exchange for human reasoning. Listen, reasoning is a good thing; but it doesn't substitue faith. It's not wrong to determine that there are walls, or that there are giants, or that there will be difficulty ahead of us for what God called us to do or to be. Yet, the Apostle Paul in essence said, *"I'm persuaded. I'm convinced that neither principalities, nor powers, nor height, nor depth shall be able to seperate us from the love of God and the power of God."*

The power of reasoning should bring us to faith. That's where reasoning should always bring us to.

Pastor Tom Carubba   93

Now, this generation of God's people in the wilderness, it was their human reasoning that led them to despair; reasoning didn't move them to faith. Reasoning didn't move them to say, *"Yes! It's true; but God said this is our inheritance! So let's go in; let's go get it; let's take it, fight for it."* They had to fight for it; the enemy is not just going to lay down; the land wasn't going to come to them, and they had to go towards the land. There's a forward motion that has to be done!

Look at the armor of God. Every piece of the armor of God covers the front of the body, nothing covers the back. WHY? Because the man and woman of God is never to be in retreat. We are always to be moving forward, pressing ahead and pushing forward.

God help us in this nation. God help us in the church. There have been too many years in the house of God where many have abandoned faith for human reasoning. We have abandoned the reproach of Christ for a social acceptability. We wanted a Christianity that was socially acceptable; that everyone would like us and for no one to laugh at us. We don't want anyone saying that we are out of our minds because we desire to be socially accepted.

If we want to be socially acceptable, we then must abandoned the cross; the preaching of the cross - which is foolishness to those who are perishing. We have abandoned the blood of Jesus. We have abandoned God's divine order. We have abandoned the things of God. We have abandoned the prayer meeting in the house of God in exchange for social acceptability.

Pastor Tom Carubba

What has been the cost to the church of Jesus Christ to be socially acceptable? We went from a God-centered faith to a man-centered faith. We've allowed millions babies to be slaughter in abortion mills. We went from being a threat to the powers of darkness to being active participants in darkness. We have lost our influence, our position and our voice in society.

You have to ask yourself, "When did Jesus stop being enough? When did obedience become an option?" Have we abandoned the seeking of God's leading for gratification of self? Much of the church's theological focus has shifted to the subject of SELF. For example: How we can become a wonderful self? How we can we become a new self? How we can become a glorified self; and many subject along these lines have become our modern theology.

Have you noticed that much of what is preached from the pulpits in American churches, can't even be preached in many places in the world? I'm talking about places where Christians are *literally* suffering and experiencing hard times as they are being thrown into prisons for their faith?

Think of the countries where Christian leaders and pastors are thrown into prison, beaten, and tortured for their faith. Try to tell them that God has come to give them a better personality; a better car and shinning teeth! Try and tell them about gold dust falling and feathers from angels showing up. What kind of response do you think they would give you? I'm telling you that these kinds of teachings and preachings, have bought nothing but weakness to the people of God and death to this nation!

Death in our churches didn't have to happen if the men and women, mainly pastors, who stood in pulpits in the churches today, had been calling the people to repentance, faith, prayer, and missions. I'm telling you, this would not have happened in our churches and nation.

Families are being torn apart and destroyed right before our eyes. The concept of family, the structure of family, God's order for the family is crumbling today as we speak.

According to statistics of the Centers for Disease Control and Prevention: 38,364 suicides in 2010; for young people 15-24 years old, suicide is the third leading cause of death. Our young people are facing hopelessness like never before!

There's no safe place anymore. There's violence everywhere: violence in malls, in offices, in churches, in schools – nothing is safe anymore in our nation!

The conclusion is this: there are things that are not up for discussion, they are not up for debate. America is dying, and it's dying on our watch. It's dying morally, dying socially, dying politically, and dying spiritually. America is on life support and it's dying on our watch!

Now, let me say to you that I have seen in God's Word, where the Lord always came to a group of people who were seeking Him; it shows me how they were given a chance to experience the true life that Jesus offers. This life will not just be a blessing to us, but it will bring freedom to many others.

Another Generation

It's been forty years in the wilderness; forty years of death, hopelessness, destruction, and decay. It's time to wake up! Somebody, somewhere has to wake up! We have to wake up and realize that with churches on just about every street corner, our country is dying. Somebody has to wake up and realize we have to get back to the House of God and BUILD the HOUSE and pray and act like we really care about our future. God help us to wake up before it's too late!

How dark does darkness have to be or how wicked, does the violence have to be? How bad does perversion have to get? How broken does society have to get, before somebody, somewhere, for the sake of the name of Jesus, and for the salvation of men and women to raise up and say, "Enough of this?"

Are you this generation that will rise up? Someone has to say, *"I'm going in, I'm going to possess what is mine. For the glory of God and the salvation of men and women, I'm going to be a testimony for God in my generation."*

The Requirement

"Every commandment which I command you today you must be

careful to observe, that you may live and multiply, and go in and possess the land of which the Lord swore to your fathers." (Deuteronomy 8:1)

For us to rise up, it requires something from us. It requires a willingness to obey God. If the willingness is not there, then there's no reason to go forward. In our heart, in our mind we have to get to the place where it's, *"Lord, I don't know every path ahead of me, but I know You have something for my life; I know what You have for my life will bring honor to Your name!"*

It won't be easy! You might be slandered, mocked, misunderstood, laughed at, and have difficulty. *"God, if You speak to us, we will follow You, not in our strength because our strength will give out; but we will lift up our hands and allow You to lead us. Take us wherever you need to; even places that we didn't want to go! We are not willing that this nation and these people die in their sin. God raise up a testimony for the honor of Your name and do it in our church and among Your people!"*

Can you say, wherever you might be right now, *"God, send an awakening, even if it's only me!"* That must be the cry of our hearts. *"Even if it's only me that wakes up spiritually and lays hold of Your throne – even if I'm the only one in my family, my workplace or city. God, You have proven throughout history that all it takes is one person to make a difference: a difference in a family, a city, a workplace, a nation and in You church!"*

Throughout history God has proven it; otherwise, everything we've studied was all for nothing! We study about Esther, Nehemiah, Gideon, Moses, Deborah, and all the heroes of faith. God has shown us that He can take the young, He can take the old, He can take the educated and uneducated. He can take anybody that says, "Here am I Lord, use me for Your glory."

The first requirement is to remember how faithful God has been. The Word of the Lord in Deuteronomy 8:2 says, **"And you shall remember that the Lord your God led you all the way these forty years in the wilderness, to humble you and test you, to know what was in your heart, whether you would keep His commandments or not."**

You can look back at your life; I can look back at my life and I can say it has not been easy; but God has been faithful. Everyone reading this book has had hard times and maybe are presently going through hard times; but you're still standing, still fed, still clothed and still here! God has been faithful and we must remember how faithful He has been; or we will lose our courage for our dreams and for where He is leading us.

The second requirement is difficult times. Deuteronomy 8:3 says: **"So He humbled you, allowed you to hunger, and fed you with manna you did not know nor did your fathers know, that He might make you know that man shall not live by bread alone; but man lives by every word that proceeds from the mouth of the Lord."**

God didn't allow us to rise up in arrogance and pride. He didn't allow us to boast in ourselves. This whole time, God was training another generation. Some of us will now see how everything we've went through; how all our suffering will make sense now. He has been getting us ready. The reason you are sitting here today, is because God's Word has kept you. You may say, "I don't know how I paid my bills, but I did. I don't know how the refrigerator got full with food, but it did. I don't know how I got through the valley of the shadow of death, but I did."

God has led each of us through seasons in our lives; yes, seasons where we didn't know how we were going to go forward; yet God, gave a word; and it was upon that word, that we were able to see another day. You caused us to find out that man doesn't live by his own resources, but by the very words that have come from You.

Do you see that in all these days, God was working faith in our heart? You're still here living by the Word of God.

The third requirement is God's covering. Then we come to, Deuteronomy 8:4: **"Your garments did not wear out on you, nor did your foot swell these forty years."** Our covering has not faded. We are declared clean by a holy God. We are sons and daughters of God in spite of our troubles, failures, trials or questions.

When it says that your foot did not swell, this means that our strength will not give out. The face of God still shines upon you in spite of your difficulties. God looks at us and calls us sons and daughters. Jesus is still at the right hand of God speaking your name and receiving you. The covering has not grown dim.

The fourth requirement is discipline. In Deuteronomy 8:5, it says: **"You should know in your heart that as a man chastens his son, so the Lord your God chastens you."** You must know that God disciplines us for our good. The words that are being spoken are being spoken to another generation, the children of those, who by human reasoning made a choice not to go into the promise land, but this generation realized that God had to discipline them so that they could be a partaker of His holiness.

There are times when you say, "God, is this really necessary?" Yes it is. It's necessary so that our dependence upon God develops.

The fifth requirement is to fear the Lord. Deuteronomy 8:6 says, **"Therefore you shall keep the commandments of the Lord your God, to walk in His ways and to fear Him."**

When we fear the Lord and have a holy reverence for God - the Lord wil bring us to a place of spiritual strength. It's a place that h*olds firm* when we're up and when we're down! You can overcome mountains and not get caught up in pride. You can go through valleys and not be overcome with despair. We're going to go through difficult days; but God says, "I'm going to give you strength that will hold firm!"

Deut. 8:7-9 **"For the Lord your God is bringing you into a good land, a land of brooks of water, of fountains and springs, that flow out of valleys and hills; a land of wheat and barley, of vines and fig trees and pomegranates, a land of olive oil and honey;" a land in which you will eat bread without scarcity, in which you will lack**

nothing; a land whose stones are iron and out of whose hills you can dig copper."

God will bring you and I to a place in Christ, a place of anointing, a place of provision, and a place of dreams. God says I'm taking you to a place of promise that's new and fresh every morning; something that can only come from God.

Do you remember the hymn, *Great is Thy Faithfulness?* Do you recall the words where it says, "Morning by morning new mercies I see." Morning by morning, new forgiveness. Morning by morning, God will make me into the person He called me to be!

In the verse above in Deuteronomy, it says, **"a land whose stones are iron and whose hills you can dig,"** meaning that it's a land where labor increases strength and trials increases the treasures of Christ. It's a place where we're not pushed back by opposition. We have confidence in the promises of God. God has promised to make me what I never could be. God has promised to take me where I could never go. God has promised to give me what I could never possess. God will do it for the glory of His name. That means that my life and your life, will be a testimony, a witness to all around us!

Will You Be this Generation?

You might not be the strongest, not the wisest, not of noble birth, or the individual with a dozen certificates on a wall. You're just an ordinary person of faith that says, *"God, here I am; and if You can take my little lunch and multiply it and feed thousands, I ask You to do it – to do in my life what only You can do."*

You might be saying to yourself, *"Pastor, you don't know. I've got giants in my life. Giants of fear, of depression, of worry, of lying voices, of regrets of how I lived my life. All these giants are stronger than I am!"* But know that none of those things are stronger than God!

Today I want to tell the Lord: *"Let's go in, I'm going to get what is mine and I don't care who stands in the way. God. I will make You this promise: I will not glorify myself; I will glorify some church; I will not glorify some preacher; I will not glorify my own human effort; but I will say of You O God, I will give You glory."*

God is the only One that could have taken you through; yes, through all the floods, the trials, the difficulties. He is the only One who brings strength out of weakness, joy out of sorrow, beauty out of ashes, HE'S THE ONLY ONE WHO COULD DO THIS!

"When you have eaten and are full, then you shall bless the Lord your God for the good land which He has given you." (Deuteronomy 8:10)

You shall bless the Lord because it is God's words that saves, that heals, that delivers, that sets free, and creates life.

We are another generation. The nation has come to a stop. The only hope for this country is the church of Jesus Christ. There is no other hope for man. God is extending an invitation to you and me - to get up and possess all that is ours through Jesus Our Lord!

Ministry Information

Hosanna World Changers is a church with a God-given vision to reach the lost, disciple those who are being saved, and release God's servants [those being equipped] into the work of ministy. It is our desire to reach both the lost in our community and around the world.

For more information regarding our ministry, please email us at:

tcarubba@hosannawc.com

Or call our offices at: *(956) 831-5750*

Our ministry & church are located at:

Hosanna World Changers
2400 Dr. Hugh Emerson Rd.
Brownsville, Texas 78526

www.ingramcontent.com/pod-product-compliance
Lightning Source LLC
Chambersburg PA
CBHW071019120626
46546CB00003B/1164